Discover
Your
Best Possible
Future

Campus Life Books

Discover Your Best Possible Future

Diane Eble and Richard Hagstrom

A DIVISION OF CTI
CampusLife
BOOKS

ZondervanPublishingHouse
Grand Rapids, Michigan
A Division of HarperCollins*Publishers*

Dɪꜱᴄᴏᴠᴇʀ Yᴏᴜʀ Bᴇꜱᴛ Pᴏꜱꜱɪʙʟᴇ Fᴜᴛᴜʀᴇ

Copyright ©1993 by Diane Eble, Richard Hagstrom and Campus Life Books, a division of CTi.
All rights reserved.

Published by Zondervan Publishing House, 5300 Patterson S.E., Grand Rapids, MI 49530
Requests for information should be addressed to: Zondervan Publishing House
Grand Rapids, Michigan 49530

Library of Congress Cataloging-in-Publication Data

Eble, Diane.
    Discover your best possible future : a step-by-step guide to choosing a college, a major,
a career / by Diane Eble and Richard Hagstrom.
        p.   cm.
    ISBN 0-310-54491-2 (paper)
    1. College, Choice of — United States.   2. Vocational guidance — United States.
3. College student orientation — United States.
I. Hagstrom, Richard. II. Title.
LB2350 . 5 . E25   1993
376.1'942 —dc20   92-45061
                                                                                CIP

Interior designed by Thomas Moraitis, Cᴀᴍᴘᴜꜱ Lɪꜰᴇ Mᴀɢᴀᴢɪɴᴇ
Cover designed by Cindy Davis

Printed in the United States of America

93   94   95   96   97   /CH/   10   9   8   7   6   5   4   3   2   1

Acknowledgments

Books are rarely written without help and input from other people. The authors would like to thank the people whose insights and feedback have helped us to develop this material.

Both authors are grateful to Dr. Bruce Barton, Dave Veerman, and Jim Galvin of the Livingstone Corporation for their valuable insights and feedback in developing this book. An especial thanks to Bruce from Dick for helping to hone the assessment guides in these pages, and for all the support and feedback he's given for many years.

Diane would like to thank Tim Stafford, who was a continual source of encouragement as he lent his expert editorial skills to this book. Thanks, Tim, for being a friend and a mentor over the years.

The authors also thank all the people who shared their Positive Experiences and worked through the process to prove that the Green Light Concept really does help people.

Contents

ing her own apartment "now that she's 18 and almost out of

Introduction

"What do you want to be when you grow up?" You have probably heard this question many times in your life so far. And when you were a kid, the answer was easy. "I'm going to be president." "I'm going to be a fireman." "I'm going to be a lawyer." The sky was the limit, and the question didn't press any panic buttons.

Now much lesser but related questions can cause panic as you get closer to that time when you are grown up. Are you going to go to college? Where? What kind of school? If not college, what kind of training will you seek? What will your college major be? What kind of job are you looking for? How will you know that the profession you choose now, when you're a teenager, will provide satisfaction and the kind of life you want when you're 30?

Even more important: Where does God's guidance fit in? How will you know you are choosing God's best for you? Do you just "know," or should you wait for a sign, or is there some process you must follow?

This book will help you find answers to all of these questions. We wrote it because we personally know a lot of young people who are struggling with these issues. We also know a lot of adults who are either unhappy in their jobs or are floundering because they made some bad decisions early in life. (Some experts say that 50 to 80 percent of working Americans are in the wrong jobs.) We'd like to spare you this kind of pain.

Both authors also enjoy their work very much and would like to help other people find the kind of job satisfaction they experience. Work can be fun—if the work matches what you like to do. What's even better, doing what you like to do is more likely to lead to success, because people excel at what they enjoy doing.

Maybe you've taken tests already that are supposed to help you figure out what you're suited for. Such tests have their place, but we believe that only you can decide what gives you satisfaction—and what gives you satisfaction is what you'll enjoy doing and be successful at.

So this book won't offer any "tests" in it. It will, however, give you clear guidance as you think your way through some important questions.

One way we'll do this is by guiding you through several simple charts that will literally help you see where your natural strengths lie. Here, at a glance, are the charts you will find throughout this book:

The Self-Assessment Guide

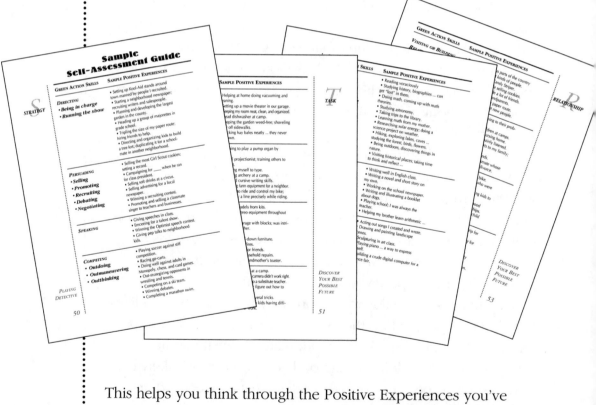

This helps you think through the Positive Experiences you've already had and begin to group those experiences into a pattern.

Action Skills Assessment

You will look at what you did in each Positive Experience and, by filling out the grid, be able to quickly see which skills you used the most.

Satisfaction Assessment

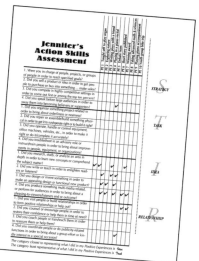

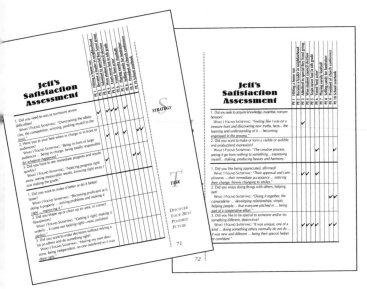

By looking at what was satisfying about each Positive Experience, you will further pinpoint what elements should be present in your future work.

As you work through these charts, you'll discover some amazing truths about yourself. These truths will help you decide not only what kind of career you want, but how that career fits into the kind of lifestyle you'd ideally like for yourself. And while nobody ever reaches his or her ideal, most of us feel reasonably content when we come close. This book will, we trust, first help you to envision the kind of life and work you want, and then give you all the tools you need to go out and make it happen, each step of the way.

What About Your Future?

WHEN YOU THINK ABOUT YOUR FUTURE, how do you feel? Scared? Excited? Bored?

Each of the following students faces a dilemma in making plans for the future. See if you recognize yourself in their stories.

Jennifer: Overwhelmed by the Options

It was fall and time for the annual career day at Central High. Jennifer felt confused but excited. So many things sounded interesting that her head began to spin. She traveled from booth to booth, picking up literature.

Her friend Melinda met her afterward for lunch. "So, Jen, did you find out what you want to be when you grow up?" she teased.

"No, not at all!" Jennifer said in mock despair. "I'm more confused than ever. What do you think: Should I go into law because I like to debate things, should I

become a pharmacist because I like math and science and it pays well, should I become a teacher because I like learning and kids, or should I become a journalist because I like to write?"

"Become a lawyer," Melinda said. "That way when I need to sue somebody, I'll know who to go to. Plus, you'll make a lot of money."

"I want to really influence people, change the world," Jennifer said. "Make a difference in some way. Do you think law would really do that? Maybe I should become a doctor. Then again,

DISCOVER YOUR BEST POSSIBLE FUTURE

13

*Looking
again
at all the
interesting
options, she
felt more
confused
than ever.*

there's music. How could I have forgotten about music? Maybe I should be a music teacher."

"Nah, that doesn't pay anything," Melinda said.

"And what are you going to do?" Jennifer asked.

"Go to an Ivy League school, then go on for my M.B.A. and become a big-wig executive on Wall Street or something," Melinda said breezily.

"That sounds like a lot of schooling."

"So does becoming a doctor or a lawyer," Melinda said.

"I know. I guess business is one of the few areas that doesn't really interest me," Jennifer said. "But what if you find some handsome, rich, fascinating guy in grad school? Would you marry him and continue your career?"

"Of course," Melinda said.

"What about having kids?"

"I probably don't want kids. But if I did, I'd probably put them in a day care center. What's the big deal? Jen, lighten up! You think too much about things."

"I know," Jennifer said with a sigh. "It's just that I know too many people who don't like what they're doing with their lives, and I don't want that to happen to me. And too many things sound possible to me. I just don't know how to narrow

things down." She bit into an apple and chewed reflectively.

Melinda said, "I don't really know what I want to do either. But I do know I want a serious career, and I probably will get an M.B.A. Right now, I'm concentrating on my grades and on getting into the best school I can."

"That's a good idea," Jennifer said, "but it seems like I should have some idea what I want to do before I choose a school, or I may end up wanting to major in something that school doesn't offer." Another friend sat down with them, and the conversation turned toward the speech project due next hour.

Later that day, in her room, Jennifer spread out the literature she'd picked up that day from the career booths. Looking again at all the interesting options, she felt more confused than ever.

Just then the youth director of her church called. "Hi, Jennifer, how are you?" Tom asked.

Before she knew it, Jennifer was telling Tom how confused she was about her future. "I pray about what I should do," she told Tom, "but I'm still confused." Tom suggested they meet together to talk further about how God guides a person in major decisions like the direction of one's life.

Sorting Through the Options

Did you see yourself in Jennifer at all?

Many students, like Jennifer, feel overwhelmed by the number of choices that seem open to them. They have lots of interests and do fairly well in school. They've heard all their lives that "if you work hard, you can succeed in anything," so the field seems wide open. Making a career choice feels scary. Jennifer was afraid that if she chose law, she'd later find out that she hated it after all and music was the route she should have taken.

A further complication, for Jennifer and other Christians, is the desire to do what God wants. It wasn't enough for Jennifer to simply choose a career that would please her; she wanted to please God, to make sure her life made a difference. She had a set of values, shaped by her faith, that urged her to do something significant with her life.

Pressure from other people can also confuse the issue. In Jennifer's case, the pressure was subtle, and it came from her peers. Jennifer was in a program that offered "accelerated" classes, and many of her friends, like Melinda, had their eyes on an Ivy League college and a high-powered career making big bucks after graduation. Jennifer couldn't help being affected by the values of those around her.

Another student, Ryan, also felt pressure about his future direction, but not from friends. And unlike Jennifer, his problem was too few options. At least, that's what it seemed like to him as he browsed through the offerings during Career Day.

Ryan: If Not College, What Do I Do?

The first booth Ryan stopped at on Career Day was for car mechanics. "I like to fix up cars," he said. "What kind of a living does a mechanic make?"

"Not a bad one," the man said. He was of medium height, but Ryan noticed his hands. They were huge. And the grease still outlined the man's fingernails. "What have you done on cars already?"

"Oh, I do all the maintenance on my parents' cars. Did a brake job for my dad once. I'm now fixing up a motorbike I bought—a 1972 650-cc Triumph. Got it for $800, put in a new engine—hope to get about $2,000 for it when I'm done. And I have a '73 Chevy Nova I fixed up."

"Not bad," said the man. "That's a good start. Then you need to go on and get some training in auto mechanics."

"You mean there's a school for that?"

"Sure. You can take courses at a community college, or hook up with a training program from Toyota or General

Motors or another car company. Or," the man said with a laugh, "you can come work for me and I'll train you."

"Serious?"

"Well, I don't need anybody right now, but sometimes we get a lot of cars in and I like to have people I can call to come in. How good are you in math?"

"Math?" asked Ryan. "Would I need math?"

"Sure. Lots of problems require math skills. I take it math isn't your thing. Well, that's not the end of the world. The main thing is that you can figure out how things work. Hey, good luck, kid."

"Yeah, thanks," Ryan said. He moved on to another booth.

Architect. That might be interesting. He browsed through the materials on the table while listening to the architect talk to another student. Uh oh, too much schooling. And you have to be good in math for that, too. Ryan moved on. Computer programming? *Boring*! he thought. What about carpentry?...

"How was the career fair?" Ryan's dad asked him as they sat down to supper that night.

"Oh, it was OK. I talked to a mechanic."

"Come on, Ryan, you know you won't get anywhere in life if you don't go on to college. Get a good education. You need at least a bachelor's degree to get a decent job. You think just because you mess up the driveway with old cars and grease that you can make a living at it?"

"Some people obviously do," Ryan said.

"Look, will you at least consider some colleges? We can sit down together and go through *Barron's Guide* to see what different colleges have to offer."

"Dad, let's be real. My grades are mostly C's. I didn't do great on the SAT—"

"You can always take it over."

"Yeah, I know, but why should I think I'd do any better?"

"Because you're more experienced at it," his dad said. "And I was thinking, I found out about a course you can take that's supposed to help you boost your SAT scores. I'll pay for it."

"Dad, I just can't see myself going through another four years of school. At this point, you should feel lucky if I graduate."

"We're not talking about my future, Ryan, this is your life we're talking about. Don't you care about your own future?" Ryan felt trapped. He cared, but he was scared, deep down. He knew college wasn't for him. He hated school. Why couldn't his father see that?

"Look, Ryan," his dad said when Ryan didn't answer, "I know a man who helps people figure out what they want to do with their lives. His name is Dick Hagstrom. It would take a little work on your part, but would you be willing to sit down with him and work with him? I'll pay for it."

"OK," Ryan said, still not looking up at his dad. He felt some stirring of hope. *Maybe this Hagstrom guy will help Dad to see how unrealistic it is for me to think about college,* he thought. *And maybe he'll have some ideas about what I can do.*

Ryan had heard so often that "you can't get anywhere without at least a college education" that he secretly did worry about his future. It was difficult for him, however, to think too much about it. It made much more sense to him to try just to make it through this year to graduation; surely something would turn up after that....

Finding Hope

Is a college education necessary for everyone? Not necessarily, though you couldn't convince Ryan's dad of that. His dad has a Ph.D. in chemistry and is a successful researcher at a major oil company. He's always assumed his son would go on to college, and he is prepared to pay for it.

But while college may not be the right route for everyone, nowadays everyone does need some sort of post-high-school training. The world is changing fast, and without further training, you really are limiting your options.

Ryan couldn't picture himself getting through four more years of school. And for what? Why should he waste his time and his dad's money on four more years of schooling when he wasn't sure what he wanted to do?

Ryan felt hopeless about his future, but he didn't need to. Once he discovered the key to his future, he became excited about the possibilities before him.

Wendy, like Ryan, didn't like school. Unlike Ryan, she wasn't particularly worried about the future, assuming it would take care of itself somehow.

Wendy: I'm Sick of School

Wendy didn't attend Career Day. Somehow she was too busy with friends. That night in her room, her friend Nicole asked as she plopped down on Wendy's bed, "So, Wendy, are you going to go to the college fair next week?"

"I'm not sure yet," Wendy answered. "I don't know about this whole college thing. My grades aren't great, and I didn't do great on the PSAT, either. To tell you the truth, I'm not sure I'm college material, as they say. I'm sick of school. I'm thinking of taking some time off to work for a while."

"What do your parents think of that?" Nicole asked.

Wendy said, "Oh, they're really pushing me to go on to school. You know, the old, 'You'll never get a decent job without at least a college education' routine."

"They're probably right, though," Nicole said. "Have you seen Mrs. Hartwell yet?"

"No, I'm supposed to set up an appointment soon with the guidance office. Just got a note the other day."

"I talked with her," Nicole said. "She's real nice. Helped a lot. I think you should go see her. They have all sorts of stuff in that office to help you figure out what to do. In fact, I thought it was kind of fun. You can take these tests and stuff that help you figure out what you'd like to do. Then they can match you up with different schools through a computer. You just punch in the kinds of things you want in a school, and then the computer spits out a list of schools that have what you want."

Wendy picked up an emery board and began to file her nails. "My trouble is, I just don't care much for school," she said. "You know, sitting in a classroom, then sitting around doing homework. It's driving me crazy now. I'm not sure I can do it for the rest of this year, let alone four more after that. I want to be out with people, doing stuff now. That's why I'm thinking of getting a job at a clothing store or something. You know how much I like to shop. Maybe if I get a job at a Nordstroms, I can get a good discount on their clothes plus help other people pick out clothes."

"Well, maybe you can do that while you're still in school," Nicole said. She picked up a magazine and started flipping through it. "I just know I get paranoid when I think about the future. What if I can't get a decent job? I know I'd hate doing some mindless office work. I want a job that's real interesting. And one that will make me lots of money," she added. "Look at this outfit! Would someone really wear that?" she asked, showing Wendy the magazine ad.

Wendy laughed, and their talk turned to fashion.

Are You a Procrastinator?

"I'll think about that tomorrow." Do you remember the famous line from *Gone with the Wind*? Maybe it worked for Scarlett, but it probably won't work for Wendy.

Wendy didn't want to think about her future because she didn't like school. She, like Ryan and his dad, assumed that "future" equaled "college" and four more years of school. Knowing only that she didn't want to go on to school, and not being much of a planner anyway, Wendy figured she'd find something somehow.

Wendy had no idea of her own strengths, or even that her tendency not to plan would be an important factor to know about herself. A senior in high school, she had no definite plans after graduation. Her guidance counselor was concerned about her. Her parents were, too. They kept dropping hints about her find-

school." Wendy thought her own apartment would be great—she could then have her friends over as late as she pleased. She figured something would turn up at the last moment.

Wendy and Ryan faced a common problem: They didn't know what they wanted to do after graduation. In contrast, Jeff, a senior in high school, had always known what he wanted to do. At least he had a dream that drove him, that of becoming a professional football player. But an injury in his junior year shattered that dream.

Wendy and Ryan faced a common problem: They didn't know what they wanted to do after graduation.

Jeff: Unexpected Change of Plans

Studying for his calculus test, all Jeff could think about was Homecoming. The game. It would be a big game. Their rivals were undefeated so far. He should be playing. If he hadn't wrecked his knee last year, he would be. He had been the star quarterback. Coach Marin thought he had a decent chance at a football scholarship. Recruiters would certainly be at the homecoming game. But none of that mattered anymore.

It had been so senseless, the injury. During practice, in a driving drill, his cleat caught in a tuft of grass just as he let up with his partner. Somehow Jeff got turned 180 degrees, and the other guy fell on top of him. Jeff will never forget the snapping sound he heard as he went down. When he tried to stand, his knee felt like water.

After many X-rays and visits to a specialist, the verdict came down: Unless he wanted to be a cripple before he was 30, he could never play football again. It was a bitter pill to swallow; football had been his life all through high school.

Now Jeff found himself floundering. His grades had improved somewhat, but lately he'd been finding it hard to get motivated. He'd always dreamed of winning a scholarship to some school and playing football. Now that his dream was shattered, he didn't know quite how to rebuild his life. It was time to start applying to colleges, and he couldn't think where to begin.

He'd poured himself into some other interests, trying to keep busy. He was a leader in his youth group. He sang in a band. Worked on the yearbook staff. Yet none of those things replaced sports in his life. The doctor said he could still play on a very limited basis, and sometimes he threw the ball around with some of the guys from his neighborhood. But it wasn't competing, and that's what Jeff had always enjoyed.

Jeff got up and sharpened his pencil. He was thirsty, so he went downstairs to get a Coke from the refrigerator. Flopping down in a chair in the family room, he noticed the stack of college catalogs. He sighed. He'd have to make an appointment with Mrs. Hartwell, the school guidance counselor, real soon. Maybe she could help him sort out his scattered thoughts.

Last year they had looked into schools that had good football teams and might offer scholarships; now all that had changed. He'd need to start over, with different criteria. Think about a major, look at things from a totally new angle. And now that there was no hope of a football scholarship, he'd have to find a way to pay for college....

When Life Throws a Curveball

As Jeff discovered, even when we make plans, life has a way of throwing us curveballs that demand we rethink our plans. Maybe for you it's that your dad got laid off and college suddenly seems hopelessly out of reach financially. Or you weren't accepted at the school of your choice and you wonder if your future will be forever compromised.

Take heart. What you will learn about yourself as you work through this book will equip you to take such changes in stride. You'll discover there are more options out there than you may have thought.

Maybe getting to college is your main concern right now. Certainly that involves a series of major decisions that must be carefully made. But once there, you'll be faced with still other crucial decisions, as Charlene and Matt discovered.

Charlene: College Isn't What I Expected

Charlene made it a point to come home the weekend after Homecoming at her Christian college. She needed to talk to her parents.

A junior in college, Charlene had decided to major in counseling and social work. But she hated college.

Hated her courses.

"Mom and Dad, I need to talk to you about something," she said. Her parents noted the serious tone in her voice. Her mom got up and turned off the TV.

Charlene sat down in the loveseat and turned to her parents. She took a deep breath. "I don't know how to tell you this. But I hate school. I'm seriously considering dropping out. I don't think I should waste your money anymore. I know how expensive it is, and I just don't like it. If I drop out right now, I'll get a refund on my tuition for the semester."

"But your grades are OK. I never knew you hated it so much," her father said. "What seems to be the problem?"

"I don't know. I just don't like the courses at all. I mean, I like the school, and I'd sure miss my friends. But college is not like I thought it would be. It's all just reading and writing papers and taking exams...I'm just not sure I can, or should, go on."

"Well, Charlene, dropping out of college is a very big step," her mother said. "I don't think you should do it until we talk more about what really is going on here. You need to think about exactly what it is you don't like about school, and let's see if there are any other solutions." Charlene agreed to think more about it, and they would talk again tomorrow.

Where Do You Go for Help?

Charlene was wise to talk to her parents before she made a big decision like dropping out of college. She needed someone to help her sort through her feelings about school, her expectations of what college would be like. She needed someone to help her reconnect with her dreams for her future and with the things that had given her satisfaction before.

As you think through your future, we encourage you to find a person whom you trust, who knows you well, to commit him or herself to working through the process with you. It may be a parent, a close relative, a youth worker, a guidance counselor, a pastor, or an older sibling or friend. Your helper should have a copy of this book and work through it with you.

A word of warning: Make sure you choose someone who is able to let *you* make the decisions. Matt, for instance, should probably choose someone other than his father to help him work through the crisis facing him.

Matt: Father Knows Best

Matt stared at his grades and felt the old frustration well up. What would his father say when he saw the engineering grade? *I don't care, I never wanted to be* an engineer anyway. The thought popped into his head, and he knew it was true. In his heart of hearts, Matt didn't give two cheeseburgers about engineering. He wanted to be a math teacher.

His father had laughed at him the first time he had mentioned that. "A math teacher! You can't even make a living at that anymore. Be an engineer. You'll be able to put those math skills to good use. Plus you'll be able to make a decent living." It had made sense to Matt. He did

like math. He did want to make a good living. So he went to the state university and planned to major in engineering.

All had gone fairly well for the first two years, when he was basically taking courses to fulfill academic requirements. But now in his junior year, he was concentrating on his major and finding his engineering courses not only difficult, but uninteresting. The C-minus for Engineering 101 did not surprise him. But it would disgust his father. How could he face his dad with these grades?

You Can't Get There From Here

We want to warn you right now: There are a lot of roads into the future that people try to take, but many lead to dead ends. Matt's dad felt that since Matt enjoyed math and did well in it, he should choose a career that used math and paid well. But such thinking is too general. A math teacher and an engineer both need to use mathematics, but each career also calls for other skills that are very different. Teaching requires interpersonal and communication skills; engineering calls for mechanical skills and abstract thinking.

There's lots of advice out there about how to choose a career; some of it is helpful, a lot is misleading. Which of the following common pieces of advice sounds familiar? Check those you think are true.

❑ "You can be and do whatever you want to. All it takes is training and hard work."

❑ "Find out where the most jobs are going to be in 10 years, and go for those jobs."

❑ "Get trained for something specific. A liberal arts degree will get you nowhere."

❑ "You don't need college to get a good job."

❑ "If you go to an Ivy League school, you'll automatically get a great job." (Or, "If you don't go to a great school, you won't get a good job.")

❑ "Grades determine what colleges you'll get into and what kind of job you'll get afterward."

❑ "No one knows you better than your parents. If they think you should go into a certain area, they must be right."

❑ "Career interest tests like the *Strong-Campbell Inventory* will tell you what career you ought to go into."

❑ "My parents and I can't afford an expensive college, so my only options are the state university or the community college."

❑ "Just pray about it and God will give you peace."

How many of these did you check as being true? Actually, though there is a grain of truth in each statement, they are all false. Yet a lot of people are misled by such beliefs and make poor decisions because of false or incomplete information. Perhaps that is why four out of five people now in the work force are unhappy in their jobs.

Most of these misconceptions ignore what we believe is the key to choosing a career that will provide both satisfaction and success.

Look Inside before Leaping

You already have inside you specific life skills that will point you in the right direction. Everything you need to choose a direction that's right for you. No matter who you are, we believe you have a unique set of abilities and motivations that add up to a particular design you're meant to fulfill.

Think for a minute about how you would purchase a car. You care not only about the outside—body style and color—but also the inside: the interior, how it feels (and smells), how the dashboard is laid out, etc. You may even pop the hood to look at the engine. A car is an investment of big bucks, and you want to make sure you're not throwing your money after a lemon.

Most of these misconceptions ignore what we believe is the key to choosing a career that will provide both satisfaction and success.

*The seeds
of fulfilling
work
doing
God's will
are
already
waiting
inside you;
properly
cultivated,
watered
with the
right
training
and
direction,
these
seeds will
bear a
fruit
unique to
you.*

WHAT
ABOUT
YOUR
FUTURE?

Your future also represents a major investment—the biggest you'll ever make in terms of energy, time, and money. While it's important to consider the outer factors—what kinds of jobs are going to be available, what colleges you should consider—it's also crucial to look inside yourself. Within your "body interior"—inside of you—are skills and abilities often overlooked and left undiscovered in the haste of making a decision. But these were "built in" by the One who designed you—God—and they are key to the work God has for you. He put you together in a certain way for a certain purpose. Finding out how he put you together will take you a long way toward finding out what he wants you to do with your life.

To change our metaphor, the seeds of fulfilling work doing God's will are already waiting inside you; properly cultivated, watered with the right training and direction, these seeds will bear a fruit unique to you.

You may have heard someone say, "He's not motivated." Or maybe you've even said that about yourself, or someone else has said it of you. But what does it mean? Usually "lack of motivation" refers to being unmotivated in certain areas of life.

Ryan and Wendy weren't motivated about school. But Ryan was very motivated when it came to fixing up old cars. And Wendy was always motivated to shop and had a knack for putting together interesting outfits on a shoestring budget.

The truth is we're all motivated in certain areas and unmotivated in other areas. A person who seems totally unmotivated just hasn't found, or valued, the areas he or she is motivated to do.

We all also have certain abilities, things we find relatively easy and enjoyable to do. Ryan found it easy to look at a car engine, figure out how it was supposed to work, and fix a problem or replace a part. Jeff wouldn't have the first clue what to do with an engine, nor did he care about it. Ryan enjoyed sports as well as anyone, but didn't feel the keen urge to compete that Jeff did. Nor did Ryan have the intrinsic sense of physical coordination and agility that came so naturally to Jeff.

Jennifer liked to study and learn; Wendy was bored by books. Wendy was a doer, wanting to be in the middle of the action, working with people rather than sitting at a desk.

Different abilities, different motivations. All add up to an unrepeatable combination that can lead to a number of satisfying work options.

Everyone Is Gifted

When we think of "gifted" people, we usually mean that someone has an unusual ability in some area—or even in a number of areas. Jennifer was in a program for "gifted" students. Those of us who have never been labeled "gifted" may feel we don't have much to offer. And even the so-called "gifted" may feel pressured into a career niche that isn't right for them.

According to the Bible, every person is "gifted." In 1 Corinthians 12, Paul explains that everyone has at least one gift. And every gift is important. Never believe that you aren't gifted! Other people need your unique combination of abilities and motivations. The Apostle Paul says, "Now the body is not made up of one part but of many. If the foot should say, 'Because I am not a hand, I do not belong to the body,' it would not for that reason cease to be part of the body. And if the ear should say, 'Because I am not an eye, I do not belong to the body,' it would not for that reason cease to be part of the body. If the whole body were an eye, where would the sense of hearing be? If the whole body were an ear, where would the sense of smell be? But in fact God has arranged the parts in the body, every one of them, just as he wanted them to be. If they were all one part, where would the body be? As it is, there are many parts, but one body.... Now you are the body of Christ, and each one of you is a part of it" (1 Corinthians 12:14-20, 27).

In this Bible passage, Paul is talking specifically about the church and how gifts are to be used in that setting. But we believe these principles also apply to how a person uses gifts in every area of life.

Think about Michael Jordan and the way the world has been inspired by his athletic abilities. Think about the best teacher you ever had. Think about the person who can make you feel good about yourself when you're discouraged. Think about the musicians whose music means a lot to you.

What if each of these people failed to cultivate their gifts? What if Michael Jordan, who didn't even make his high-school basketball team, had given up on basketball? What if your favorite teacher had taken a more lucrative but less personally fulfilling job? What if your favorite musician had taken someone's advice and given up music and was working as a Burger King manager?

The world would be a poorer place. *You* would be a poorer person.

The world needs your gifts! You owe it to other people, as well as to yourself, to find out what they are and use them. You have a certain design to fulfill, as unique a design as your fingerprint. Put another way, you hold the key to unlocking not only a fulfilling life for yourself, but a treasure chest of good things that will benefit others. They'll prove it to you by paying you money for what you can do well.

And you alone hold that key. No tests, no other person, can dictate what your design is. Other people can certainly help you discover what's already there, and we'll show you how. But only you can and should choose your own direction, based on your unique, God-given design.

Go for the Green

Picture this: You're going to drive a car on this journey into your future. You have the key already in hand. But you need several other things in order to complete the trip.

You must, of course, decide where you're going. We'll help you do that. Think of this book as a map that will show you how to choose your destination, how to find the route to that destination, and how to get help when you need it.

You'll also need to know how to read important signals and signs. Picture for a moment a stoplight. Remember what we said about abilities and motivations? Think of your unique set of abilities and motivations in terms of the green, yellow, and red of a traffic light.

Green stands for those areas in which you have ability and are motivated. Knowing your Green area will help you choose a career direction and figure out a major. Green means go—full speed ahead, foot on accelerator. Green is enjoyable. We'll talk about how to discover your Green in the next chapter.

On the other hand, a yellow light signals caution. *Yellow* may represent an area in which there may be some motivation but not as much ability—or vice versa, some ability with little motivation. And *red*, of course, means stop. Red and yellow represent a person's limited skills—his or her "liabilities." Yellow and red mean foot on the brake—stop rather than start. When required to use liabilities, a person slows down, delays, procrastinates.

Obviously you don't want to pursue a career in your "red" area, but it happens to people all the time. That was Matt's problem. He knew what he wanted to do—teach math—but he let his father pressure him into an area that didn't interest him—engineering. Pressure from parents or other important people can be powerful—and subtle. You may not even realize that you're operating under other people's assumptions and expectations until you face a crisis, like Charlene and Matt did.

We strongly urge you to make sure you're in the driver's seat. Your job is to listen to God's voice and follow the "map" he has given you. (You'll know how to read this "map" by the time you're done with this book.)

Only you can and should choose your own direction, based on your unique, God-given design.

DISCOVER YOUR BEST POSSIBLE FUTURE

27

*Other
people are
there to
help you
notice
some signs
along the
way that
you may
miss other-
wise—that
is their
only role.*

Invite your helper into the car, but make sure he or she understands that you're the driver. Other people are there to help you notice some signs along the way that you may miss otherwise—that is their only role. As soon as they begin to take the wheel, gently but firmly remind them that *you* are the driver.

Where Are You Now?

OK, so you've hopped into the car behind the wheel, your key is in the ignition and you're ready to roll. Before you turn that key, take a moment right now to check off your personal starting point on this journey into your future.

When I think about my future, I:

❑ Know exactly what I want to do and how to get there.

❑ Feel there are too many options and don't know how to choose.

❑ Have a general idea of what I want to do but don't know if it'll be right for me.

❑ Feel there are no good options for me.

❑ Other (explain)

What I need right now is to:

❑ Figure out a general career direction.

❑ Choose a college.

❑ Decide on further education options.

❑ Choose a college major.

❑ Understand God's will for my life.

❑ Find a job.

❑ Other (explain)

The next step is to make sure you're running on GAS. That is, you need to know your Green Action Skills—those things that come naturally to you, that you enjoy doing, and that will provide the fuel to get you where you want to go.

Let's get started!

CHAPTER 2

Looking Back at Your Future

JEFF KNOCKED ON MRS. HARTWELL'S DOOR, and at her cheerful "Come in!" he entered the guidance counselor's office and threw himself down on a chair facing her.

He had been dreading this encounter, but he knew it had to come. Putting off decisions wouldn't make things any easier. His parents were gently pressuring him to apply to college. He had no idea where to begin.

"I'm glad to see you, Jeff," Mrs. Hartwell said, smiling. "What can I do for you?"   He took a deep breath and plunged in.

"Well, you know how I had my heart set on a football scholarship. The coach had really thought I would get one. But now, with this injury, the doctors say I really shouldn't play at all. And I'm a senior now. I know I should be applying to colleges, but I don't know where I want to go or what I want to do. Football was my life, and now I have to find something else." Admitting that, Jeff felt bad all over again. His knee began to throb.

"I'm glad you're not letting this wait, Jeff. It really shows a lot of character on your part to have kept your grades up, and to not let important decisions slide."

*Positive
experiences
you've
already had
provide
important
clues to
what you'll
enjoy doing
in the
future.*

He'd never thought of it that way.

"Yeah, but I'm finding it hard to get motivated," Jeff admitted. "I go through the motions, but I really haven't found anything else I enjoy nearly so much as I enjoyed sports. That's what scares me."

Mrs. Hartwell looked at him reflectively for a moment. "You know, Jeff, maybe this injury will turn out to be a blessing in disguise," she said.

"What do you mean?" He'd already struggled with the whole question of whether any good could come of this injury—and had gotten no answers so far. His Christian friends talked about how God could work anything out for good, and he'd tried to believe that. But it was still hard. What did Mrs. Hartwell know that wasn't apparent to him?

"Well," she replied, "if football really was your life, as you say, then maybe you would have set yourself up for a major jolt if you'd continued along the path you were on. Very few people make it to the professional level. Most people who do very well in sports have to find other ways to make a living sooner or later anyway. Maybe being forced to find other interests now will benefit you more in the long run."

"I never thought of it that way," Jeff said slowly. "But I still don't know what else I want to do."

Mrs. Hartwell suggested, "Why don't we look back on what gave you satisfaction in the past. I believe positive experiences you've already had provide important clues to what you'll enjoy doing in the future. I'd like you to take this form and write down some things you've done in the past that gave you satisfaction. Then we'll get together and talk in more detail about each experience. I think you'll be encouraged about what we discover."

Jeff took the paper Mrs. Hartwell held out to him, feeling a faint stirring of hope for the first time since his injury.

Looking Back to Move Ahead

Mrs. Hartwell was right: The key to your future lies in your past. Let us explain.

If you look back over your life so far and ask yourself what positive, fulfilling experiences you've had, you should be able to name at least a few. You were born with certain abilities and motivations—the outline of your unique design. From the very beginning, there were certain things that attracted you and other things that you avoided. You have already done many things that you enjoyed and felt you did well. They may not have been achievements in the eyes of others, but as you think back over your life, certain experiences come to mind that still, for some reason, provide a sense of satisfaction to you.

In these Positive Experiences are the seeds of your future success.

Positive Experiences give a sense of accomplishment, competence, and fulfillment. That's why they serve as the basic clues to your strengths and capabilities. They are the foundation upon which the major decisions about your future should be made. And they are yours alone. That's why we say only you hold the key to your future.

Positive Experiences: Key to Your Green

Remember what we said about the traffic light? Your Green Action Skills are what you want to pursue, full speed ahead. These Green Action Skills are the GAS that will keep you going in the right direction. They are the abilities you've already used in the positive experiences that have given you a sense of fulfillment in the past. To figure out your green areas of abilities, you

Positive Experiences give a sense of accomplishment, competence and fulfillment. That's why they serve as the basic clues to your strengths and capabilities.

Everyone's
Positive
Experiences
are
different—
unique to
him or her.

need to get down on paper your Positive Experiences.

It's easy and fun to do. It doesn't require a lot of introspection. It doesn't require any knowledge of psychology, or the ability to write (though those who like to write will be able to do a lot of it if they want). What it does require is the time to sit down and think over your own past achievements.

First, take a piece of paper (or photocopy the form on page 37 and use). Divide your life in half, beginning at age five, and list five to seven positive, fulfilling experiences you've had in each time period. A Positive Experience is any past activity:

(a) you were naturally interested in;

(b) you did because you wanted to;

(c) you did fairly well (in *your* opinion).

Everyone's Positive Experiences are different—unique to him or her. Your Positive Experiences are accomplishments in your own eyes, regardless of what other people may have thought. Your achievements don't have to be earthshaking, just things that were meaningful to you. They may have occurred at school, home, a club, a job, or wherever.

As you think over your Positive Experiences, keep these things in mind:

1. People have different ways of approaching this. Some sit down and complete it all at once. Some think it over and write down a little at a time, as ideas occur to them. Others talk to people and then write. Do whatever is natural to you, but make sure that what you write are things *you* enjoyed and that *you* feel you did well, not what someone else thinks was an achievement.

2. When we say "Positive Experience" we mean something specific you did, something you accomplished. *Not:* Taking family vacations. *Rather:* Exploring new trails when our family took vacations.

3. Don't worry about whether or not you can remember your earliest experiences. You will, if you keep an open mind and don't reject something because it seems trivial. When you

remember a significant experience, write it down. Don't try to analyze or evaluate it.

4. The events may not come to mind in the order you did them. Don't worry about that. Just get them down.

5. After you list your PEs, go back and do two things:

(a) Circle the earliest three experiences.

(b) Rank them: (1) most fulfilling, (2) a little less fulfilling, etc.

Jeff found it surprisingly fun to sit down and fill out his list of Positive Experiences. Here's what he wrote:

Jeff's Positive Experiences

Period 1: Ages 5-12

Hitting a home run in Little League. (4)

Became popular and leader in our neighborhood even though we had just moved to a new area. (5)

Admitted to the Order of the Arrow, a special group within Boy Scouts. Made more badges than anyone else. (3)

Winning student council election in fourth grade. (8)

In sixth-grade gym class, my team never lost no matter what sport we played. (2)

Period 2: Ages 13-18

Voted "best actor" in sophomore English class. (9)

Getting on the football team and playing varsity. (1)

Selling candy to raise money for our youth group. (10)

Serving as president of a regional high-school church conference. (6)

Working on the school yearbook. (7)

To give you an idea of the range of Positive Experiences, let's look at what some of the people we met in the last chapter included on their lists.

Wendy's Positive Experiences

Period 1: Ages 5-12

Making two "sock babies" from Granny's scrap basket for little brother's birth. (7)

Helping my sister make paper dolls. (10)

Having the best collection of Barbie doll clothes in the neighborhood. (9)

Helping put on a muscular dystrophy carnival with my sisters. (6)

Planning a surprise party for my sister. (3)

Period 2: Ages 13-18

Cutting my sister's hair—and having her like it. (2)

My first job at a beauty salon. (8)

Designing my first dress and wearing it to a school dance. (1)

Befriending a girl in school who was not popular, and helping her become better liked. (5)

Christmas shopping with my own money, picking out just the right gifts. (4)

Ryan's Positive Experiences

Period 1: Ages 5-12

Serving as hall monitor in school. (9)

Doing geometry problems quickly. (10)

Working on my bike ... fixing it. (5)

Building a racetrack for AFX cars. (6)

Having a garage sale. "I love buying something cheap, fixing it, and then selling it at a profit." (3)

Period 2: Ages 13-18

Buying things at auctions. (8)

Working in a machine shop. (7)

Working on my car and motorcycle. (1)

Building balsa wood airplanes and rockets. (4)

Learning about combustion engines. (2)

Jennifer's Positive Experiences

Period 1: Ages 5-11

Teaching myself to play the organ. (3)

Being outdoors and exploring nature while camping with my family. (7)

Writing plays with my friend. (4)

Period 2: Ages 12-17

Being on the debate team. (6)

Having my short story published in the school journal. (1)

Winning an award for an environmental contest and going to Boston to accept it from an important statesman. (2)

Taking advanced math and sciences. (10)

Playing piano accompaniment at church. (8)

Taking a long bike trip with the youth group. (9)

Charlene's Positive Experiences

Period 1: Ages 5-12

Learning songs, acting out parts, and singing. (7)

Playing in the snow, acting out fairy tales. (8)

Performing in a grade school play. Had one of the leads. (4)

Learning to play the guitar, writing songs, and singing them in church. (5)

Period 2: Ages 13-20

Having my own singing group. (2)

Creating a folk mass. (3)

Singing weekends at a restaurant. (6)

Singing solos; I write my own songs. (1)

Matt's Positive Experiences

Period 1: Ages 5-13

Teaching my little brother how to make model airplanes. (4)

Making new friends at school when we moved. (5)

Getting a dog. (10)

Visiting an old man (former neighbor). (6)

Figuring out puzzles that no one else could get. (11)

Period 2: Ages 14-21

Tutoring fellow students in math. (1)

Leading a Bible study with two other people. (7)

Teaching a Sunday school class. (2)

Being with friends on different sports teams. (8)

Taking advanced math classes. (3)

Living with four roommates ... enjoyed working things out together. (9)

We hope you've got the idea of what Positive Experiences might look like. Remember, they must be specific things you did because they naturally interested you, things you freely chose to do, and things you did well in your own eyes.

Now, write down your own Positive Experiences. These will become a rich source of information that we'll build on for the rest of the book, so it's worth taking some time to be thorough with this process.

My Positive Experiences

Period 1: Ages ....   **Period 2: Ages** ....

Digging Deeper

Now that you've gotten your basic Positive Experiences on paper, it's time to expand on them. This will provide the gold mine of information that will tell you:

—How you like to function with others (by yourself? as a team player? as the boss? what kind of boss?)

—What you most like to work with (numbers? things? ideas? people? words? equipment?)

—What abilities you enjoy using most (analyzing? evaluating? persuading? performing?)

—What you get out of your achievements (feeling special? influencing others? building or developing?)

All this information is connected to your Positive Experiences. In order to mine this rich field of information, you need to expand a little on each Positive Experience. You need to give a little more detail about *what you did, how you did it,* and *what was satisfying about your experience.* All this can be done in a brief, casual talk we call a Discovery Conversation.

Let's take a look at how Jeff approached his Discovery Conversation. Since the earliest experiences often tell us a great deal, we'll listen in on the first three achievements Jeff listed. Then we'll look at some of the steps he and Mrs. Hartwell took, so that you will be able to get the most out of your own Discovery Conversation. In the next chapter we'll go into how Jeff might figure out what these experiences tell him about his big question: "Where do I go from here with my life?"

Jeff's Discovery Conversation

"Hi, Jeff," Mrs. Hartwell greeted him. "Do you have your Positive Experiences Listing with you?"

"Sure do," Jeff said. "It was fun filling it out."

"That's the beauty of this system," Mrs. Hartwell said. "I think you'll enjoy the Discovery Conversation for the same reason. Are you ready? I have a cassette in the recorder here, and I'll be taking notes while you talk.

"Let's start with the first Positive Experience: 'Hitting a home run in Little League.' Tell me what exactly you did in this Positive Experience."

Jeff remembered: "The pitcher pitched high, and I whaled at it, hit it real solid, saw it take off; all my teammates went crazy! I remember the smack of the bat, but I hardly felt it; it had that weightless sensation. It was an exceptional hit, a deep, long, hard hit to deepest center field. That kind of hit only happens a few times to someone at that age. It must have been like one of the top one percent of hits made in Little League. That's what the coach said, anyway. And people didn't stop talking about it for weeks."

"What was satisfying about this achievement?" Mrs. Hartwell asked.

Jeff was staring at her bookcase, a smile on his face, remembering. "It was the fulfillment of a dream," he said. "A sense of ultimate achievement—it was the kind of hit they made in the big leagues. It felt wonderful to see the ball fly off the bat, to see it going so fast and far! It also was exciting to be jogging around the bases, knowing there was no way I'd get thrown out at the plate. I knew there was no way we'd lose the game after that."

Mrs. Hartwell smiled. "OK, let's go on to the next achievement. 'Admitted to the Order of the Arrow, a special group within Boy Scouts.' How did this Positive Experience begin?"

"Well," Jeff answered, "it happened the last night of Boy Scout camp. The Order of the Arrow is a fraternal organization within Boy Scouts. You had to be chosen to be in it. It meant that you were an outstanding scout in some way.

"On that last night at camp, we didn't know who would be chosen— they called it 'tapped out.' All us boys were in a circle, it was Thursday night, we were in this circle around a fire by the lake, and the Indians who do the tapping out came in a canoe at dusk.

"The water was still, and we could see this canoe coming toward us. The Indians had torches, they were coming across the water, and the lights were getting bigger and the night darker. Then they hit shore. They were singing Indian songs, like chants, and the Indians on our side were also singing; they were calling back and forth.

"They got out of the boat and began walking over, then they circled around us. They were doing Indian dances, and wearing Indian outfits with bells, so you heard the jingling of bells and the campfire, and that was it. Then an Indian would grab a boy, jerk him around, and the chief would tap him hard on the shoulder. When I was tapped out, I remember how hard he tapped. Then they'd hand you an arrow, you would hold it out, they would push you back in and pick another person. When this was over we filed out of line, and they would come back around and you would follow them and you couldn't talk for the rest of the night. You'd go to sleep wondering what was going to happen next.

"Some time in the next month I was called to come back. In the meantime I had to carve a totem pole to bring with me. The day we were called back for an initiation, you couldn't talk all day while you worked around camp, cleaning up. You had a little piece of wood around your neck. If you talked, an older boy would put a notch in the wood. You didn't want any notches. In the evening we were given a sleeping bag, an egg, a match, and an orange—that was it. We were supposed to make a fire and cook the egg, I guess. I actually made a fire, even though the wood was pretty damp, and I cooked the egg and ate the orange. I felt like I'd really overcome the odds and learned something about survival. They dropped us off somewhere and I slept on the ground in the sleeping bag. I was pretty tired from all the work I'd done. The next day I left."

"What was fulfilling about this experience?"

"Being chosen. It meant a lot to wear that white sash with the red arrow; it said I was one of the best. The younger boys looked up to you. Also, my father was extremely proud of me. My dad had been one of the first Boy Scouts in Atwood, and he really pushed scouting. I was one of the youngest boys to be tapped out. It meant a lot to him to have me be chosen."

"Was there anything else fulfilling about this achievement?"

"Going the following summer to the

Order of the Arrow Conclave in Lincoln, Nebraska. I felt privileged to be there. I stayed in a dorm room with three other Boy Scouts, all older than me. Yet they treated me as equals. We tried foods from all over the world that the Scouts had made. I sampled fish I'd never eaten before."

Mrs. Hartwell checked the tape recorder. Plenty of tape yet. She asked, "What did you do that caused you to be chosen into the Order of the Arrow?"

"I wanted to be the best, so I worked very hard to get certain merit badges. I think the scout master thought I was on the way to being the first Eagle Scout in the troupe. (But he was wrong. I never made it that far.)"

"OK, let's go on to the next item. 'Became popular and leader in our neighborhood, even though we had just moved to a new area.' Tell me exactly what you did."

Jeff leaned back in his chair, remembering again. "My family moved to a new town just before I started third grade. I didn't know a soul. But in my neighborhood I saw another boy riding his bicycle. One day I got on my bike and rode over to his house and introduced myself. His name was Danny. We rode our bikes that day in the neighborhood, and later he invited me to play kickball with some of the kids at the end of our street.

"There were a lot of kids in our neighborhood around my age. Even though I was the new kid, pretty soon somehow people were looking to me as the leader. They just seemed to like my ideas."

Mrs. Hartwell asked, "Can you give me an example of ways you became the leader?"

"Well," Jeff said, grinning, "I remember

one time I thought it would be great to have a neighborhood carnival; I organized one and ran it and got the other kids to help. We had a lot of fun and helped raise some money."

"Any other examples?" Mrs. Hartwell asked, busily scribbling notes.

"I also was usually the captain when we would organize neighborhood games. We played a lot of things, kickball and keep-away and volleyball, soccer, touch football, and softball. My team usually won, though we wouldn't always have the same kids on the same teams."

"What was fulfilling about this Positive Experience?" Mrs. Hartwell asked.

"I just liked going from the new kid nobody knew to the one everyone looked up to," Jeff said. "I liked coming up with new ideas and being in charge and running things. I liked it when we played sports."

"OK, Jeff, let's go on to the next experience. Tell me two or three things you did when you got elected to student council in fourth grade...."

Remember, a Discovery Conversation is not a formal interview, but rather a casual time for you to tell more about what you accomplished.

In the next chapter we'll go into how Jeff might figure out how his past experiences can guide his future decisions. But before we look at that, let's go back over the steps he and Mrs. Hartwell took in his Discovery Conversation, so that you too can make the most of your Positive Experiences.

How to Do Your Discovery Conversation

Remember, the purpose of a Discovery Conversation is to tell what two or three things you did in each Positive Experience, and what was satisfying about the accomplishment. It's not a formal interview, but rather a casual time for you to tell more about what you accomplished. Here's what to do.

1. *Decide how you want to approach the Discovery Conversation.* We call it a conversation because most people find it easier to talk than to write. But if you feel more comfortable writing it out by yourself, feel free to do that. However, since there are advantages to telling it to someone, we suggest you work with another person.

Jeff, of course, saw his guidance counselor. Jennifer sat down with her youth pastor; Ryan went to Dick Hagstrom; Wendy got together with her friend Nicole; Charlene talked to her parents;

and Matt, who wasn't sure how his father might react, talked into a tape recorder, using our guidelines. (His ever-faithful Labrador listened patiently, but wasn't real quick with asking the right questions.) As we will see later, even the way you approach this task reflects your unique design.

Choose your interviewer carefully. It should be someone you trust, someone who really wants to help you discover your own way. Remember what we said earlier: It's crucial that you be in the driver's seat. Your interviewer should be someone mature enough to let you do the talking, to stick to the interviewer's guidelines faithfully. If you don't think you know any such person, follow Matt's example: Talk to yourself or your dog. Just make sure you tape the conversation—a dog may be man's best friend, but most of them are lousy note takers!

2. *Approach your interviewer.* Once you've completed your list of Positive Experiences, go to the person you'd like to conduct the conversation and give him or her a copy of your list and a copy of the guidelines on the following page. Make sure the person reads the guidelines and understands what you want.

3. *Make sure you document your Discovery Conversation.* The best way to do this is to tape it. You might also have someone take notes as you talk; that will save time later. But it should be taped as well, if at all possible.

4. *Talk about at least two or three specific things you did in each Positive Experience.* Describe everything you can remember about your part in the achievement. Focus on the details of *what* you did and *how* you did it. There are many ways to sew a dress, organize a party, or tutor a friend; how you approached the task is important. So go into detail. Act as if your interviewer is from a different planet and doesn't understand exactly how things are done in this world.

As you describe what you did, you may find yourself repeating a word or phrase. When that happens, don't be concerned or try to say it differently. Repetition is fine.

Give examples and illustrations. Talk about how you got involved, what you worked with, what you did, what you were trying to achieve. If it was a group effort, tell about what you did and what your role was.

Be subjective. Tell how it felt to you. Don't worry about modesty; you are the star player in each of these achievements. (This is what makes these Discovery Conversations so much fun! When else can you talk in such detail about things you've done that really meant a lot to you, and have someone listen in complete silence with absolutely no judging?)

5. *Be sure to describe what was fulfilling to you.* What did you enjoy doing the most in this accomplishment? Try to think of two or three things about the achievement that provided satisfaction. If there was anything you did in the accomplishment that you disliked or found distasteful, mention that too. But since we're focusing on *positive* experiences, make sure you tell what was enjoyable and fulfilling about what you did.

Before you go on to the next chapter, take some time out to fill in your Positive Experiences Form if you haven't already done so. Decide how you want to approach the Discovery Conversation. Once you have a cassette and/or notes containing the details of your accomplishments in hand, you're ready for the next big step: figuring out what it all means for your future. The fun continues!

Discovery Conversations are fun! When else can you talk in such detail about things you've done that really meant a lot to you, and have someone listen in complete silence with absolutely no judging?

Guidelines for the Interviewer

The purpose of this interview is to help the interviewee recall and explain in detail the accomplishments he or she has listed on the Positive Experiences Form. What you are after is at least two or three specific things the person did and what he or she found fulfilling about each accomplishment. As the interviewee talks, you tape what is said. (You or a third person may also take notes.) Keep in mind the following important points:

❑ *Avoid leading questions.* Do not explore areas that interest you; your role is exclusively to help the person expand on his or her Positive Experiences. At another time you may bring up what the person has said and dialogue about it. This is not a two-way conversation; you do not have to do anything but ask the questions that follow.

❑ *Avoid judging.* All people seek to fulfill their design. The means they choose may appear selfish or selfless, but what they're seeking is personal satisfaction. You are helping this individual to understand the motivation behind the achievement, so he or she will better know what exactly gives a sense of fulfillment.

To begin the interview, read the description of the person's earliest Positive Experience from the Positive Experiences Form (it should be one of the circled ones), and ask, "How did you get started in this activity?" What you're looking for are details of what the person did, how he or she went about doing it, and what was fulfilling. You might find the following questions helpful in eliciting this information:

❑ What were the specifics of what you actually did?
❑ Can you give me an illustration of what you mean by _____?

❑ Would you give me one example of that?

❑ What was your role in this accomplishment?

❑ What did you enjoy about what you did?

❑ What aspect of this activity gave you the greatest sense of personal accomplishment and reward?

❑ What would have made this activity even more rewarding for you?

❑ Were there any aspects of this activity that you disliked or found distasteful?

If you are taking notes rather than or in addition to taping the session, do the following:

❑ Note any details that describe what was actually done. You should have at least two or three verbs that recur for each experience.

❑ Note, verbatim if possible, words that reveal *an ability* ("developed," "wrote"); *a subject matter worked with* (animals, words, equipment); *whether the person interacted with others* ("did it with my sister"); *what was enjoyable* ("loved getting something all neat and straight").

❑ When an example is given, note the features the interviewee emphasized ("was considered the best"; "did it without anyone having to tell me how to"; "figured it out by myself").

❑ Take down quotes verbatim ("Teacher said, 'I never give A's, but you deserve this one' ").

❑ Note any numbers used ("saved $2,486 and bought my first car").

CHAPTER 3

Playing Detective

JENNIFER SAT DOWN ACROSS FROM TOM, her youth pastor, in the Pizza Hut booth. She had already listed her Positive Experiences and described what she did and what was satisfying about each experience. Tom had recorded the Discovery Conversation and taken notes. Now they were meeting to try to make some sense out of what it all meant.

After they ordered their pizza and Pepsi, Jennifer leaned forward and said, "It was really fun to talk about all those positive experiences. But I don't feel much closer to knowing what to do. I look at the list and still see too many different types of things."

"That's OK," Tom said. "It may not seem like there are any patterns now, but as we go through your list and compare it with some other information I have, I think it will begin to make sense to you. Let's look again at your original list of Positive Experiences...."

Tom knew how to help Jennifer because he'd been trained to know what patterns to look for. He took Jennifer through some simple but crucial steps for making sense of her Positive Experiences.

DISCOVER YOUR BEST POSSIBLE FUTURE

Let's look at how Jennifer worked through this process, step by step. Then we'll see how Jeff made sense of his Positive Experiences. Finally, we'll take *you* through the process each step of the way, and then we'll tell you what it all means for you.

Don't feel intimidated by all of the charts that follow. As you'll see, this process is not as difficult as it may seem at first glance. But it is important! It may *seem* easier to just plug some answers into a computer and let it spit out a blueprint for your life, but no computer can give you the answers that are right for you. If you want true answers, if you want a direction that is in tune with your deepest desires and unique abilities, take a bit of time to work through the process we're about to describe. You're looking for buried treasure—the unique, God-given abilities you were put on earth to use for him.

Now, let's go back and see how Jennifer discovered her Green Action Skills—those abilities she can build her future on.

Jennifer Finds Her Green Action Skills

Tom took out a stack of papers. Jennifer groaned. "Oh, oh, looks like a test!" she said.

"Take out your number two pencil. Do not open the test until I say so," Tom said in his best test proctor voice. Then he said, "No, seriously, this is just a simple tool to help you figure out what your Positive Experiences mean.

"The man who trained me, Dick Hagstrom," Jeff continued, "has worked with lots of people of all ages. He has found that one of four common threads will recur in their Positive Experiences. The things you like doing (your Green Action Skills) will tend to fall into one of the categories Dick has identified and labeled."

"I hate being labeled," Jennifer interrupted. "People have been calling me things like 'sticks' and 'bones' and 'brains' all my life."

Jennifer looked again at her Positive Experiences:
• Teaching myself to play the organ.
• Being outdoors and exploring nature while camping with my family.

Jeff agreed, "Labels are usually a pretty negative thing. But in this case, it can actually be kind of helpful. Dick's label can quickly summarize your area of strength and keep you from making a wrong turn down your career path."

"OK," Jennifer said, smiling, "so what's my label?"

"I'll let you find out for yourself," he replied. "Most of the things you did that show up in your Positive Experiences will fall into one of these four areas: Strategy, Task, Idea, or Relationship. We refer to this as S-T-I-R; it stands for what *stirs* you, the things you've done that have provided fulfillment and satisfaction.

"Here's a Self-Assessment Guide that will help you make sense of your Positive Experiences," he continued, handing her a thin booklet of eight-by-ten papers. "Open up to Step One. This is a list of sample Positive Experiences in each of the S-T-I-R categories. Take your list of Positive Experiences and compare them to this list." Jennifer looked at the list with interest. Here's what she read:

Most of the things you did that show up in your Positive Experiences will fall into one of these four areas: Strategy, Task, Idea, or Relationship.

STEP ONE. On the next page is a list of characteristics and sample Positive Experiences for each of the four categories. Look over the sample Positive Experiences and add yours to whichever categories they best fit in.

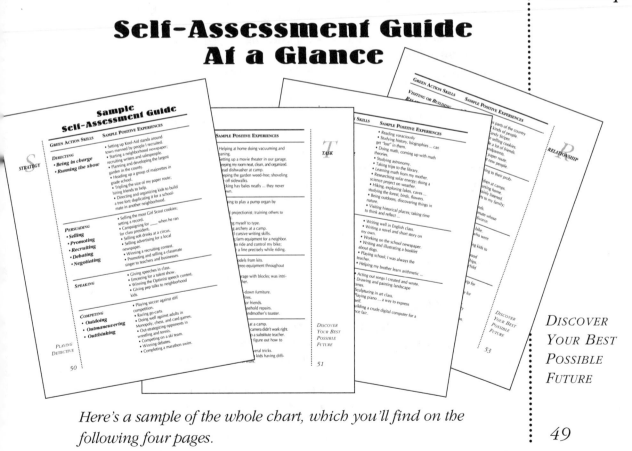

Self-Assessment Guide At a Glance

Here's a sample of the whole chart, which you'll find on the following four pages.

Sample
Self-Assessment Guide

GREEN ACTION SKILLS	SAMPLE POSITIVE EXPERIENCES
DIRECTING • *Being in charge* • *Running the show*	• Setting up Kool-Aid stands around town manned by people I recruited. • Starting a neighborhood newspaper; recruiting writers and salespeople. • Planning and developing the largest garden in the county. • Heading up a group of majorettes in grade school. • Tripling the size of my paper route; hiring friends to help. • Directing and organizing kids to build a tree fort; duplicating it for a schoolmate in another neighborhood.
PERSUADING • *Selling* • *Promoting* • *Recruiting* • *Debating* • *Negotiating*	• Selling the most Girl Scout cookies; setting a record. • Campaigning for ____ when he ran for class president. • Selling soft drinks at a circus. • Selling advertising for a local newspaper. • Winning a recruiting contest. • Promoting and selling a classmate singer to teachers and businesses.
SPEAKING	• Giving speeches in class. • Emceeing for a talent show. • Winning the Optimist speech contest. • Giving pep talks to neighborhood kids.
COMPETING • *Outdoing* • *Outmaneuvering* • *Outthinking*	• Playing soccer against stiff competition. • Racing go-carts. • Doing well against adults in Monopoly, chess, and card games. • Out-strategizing opponents in wrestling and tennis. • Competing on a ski team. • Winning debates. • Completing a marathon swim.

GREEN ACTION SKILLS	SAMPLE POSITIVE EXPERIENCES
STRAIGHTENING OUT/ORGANIZING • *Setting up* • *Arranging* • *Cleaning*	• Helping at home doing vacuuming and cleaning. • Setting up a movie theater in our garage. • Keeping my room neat, clean, and organized. • Head dishwasher at camp. • Keeping the garden weed-free; shoveling snow off sidewalks. • Stacking hay bales neatly … they never fell down.
OPERATING/HANDLING OR CONTROLLING • *Tools, equipment, vehicles* • *At a keyboard or controls*	• Learning to play a pump organ by myself. • School projectionist; training others to operate it. • Teaching myself to type. • Teaching archery at a camp. • Perfected cursive writing skills. • Operating farm equipment for a neighbor. • Learning to ride and control my bike; could follow a line precisely while riding.
REPAIRING OR ASSEMBLING/BUILDING • *Fixing* • *Constructing*	• Building models from kits. • Installing stereo equipment throughout our house. • Building a garage with blocks; was intricately put together. • Fixing clocks. • Making scaled-down furniture. • Building campfires. • Repairing toys for friends. • Doing small household repairs. • Repairing my grandmother's toaster.
TROUBLESHOOTING OR INSTRUCTING • *Advising* • *Teaching*	• Teaching archery at a camp. • Finding out why my camera didn't work right. • Being an "adviser" to a substitute teacher. • Helping my brother figure out how to operate his computer. • Teaching my dog several tricks. • Problem-solving with kids having difficulty with school work.

GREEN ACTION SKILLS	SAMPLE POSITIVE EXPERIENCES
RESEARCHING • *Studying* • *Exploring* • *Investigating*	• Reading voraciously • Studying history, biographies ... can get "lost" in them. • Doing math, coming up with math theories. • Studying astronomy. • Taking trips to the library. • Learning math from my mother. • Researching solar energy; doing a science project on weather. • Hiking, exploring lakes, caves ... studying the forest, birds, flowers. • Being outdoors, discovering things in nature. • Visiting historical places; taking time to think and reflect ...
WRITING OR *TEACHING* • *Instructing* • *Tutoring*	• Writing well in English class. • Writing a novel and short story on my own. • Working on the school newspaper. • Writing and illustrating a booklet about dogs. • Playing school; I was always the teacher. • Helping my brother learn arithmetic ...
CREATING/SHAPING/ *EXPRESSING* • *Performing* • *Making* • *Designing* • *Inventing*	• Acting out songs I created and wrote. • Drawing and painting landscape scenes. • Sculpturing in art class. • Playing piano ... a way to express myself. • Building a crude digital computer for a science fair.

GREEN ACTION SKILLS	SAMPLE POSITIVE EXPERIENCES
VISITING OR BUILDING RELATIONSHIPS • *Befriending* • *Helping*	• Traveling to various parts of the country and meeting different kinds of people. • Being a volunteer Candy Striper. • Visiting people while selling cookies. • Playing softball; made a lot of friends. • Being close to my grandparents. • Making friends on my paper route. • Going to camp to meet new people.
COUNSELING OR ENCOURAGING • *Waiting on* • *Helping*	• Talking to friends, listening to their problems. • Counseling crippled children at camps. • Visiting the elderly at a nursing home. • Helping a sickly aunt; I mainly listened. • Making and serving desserts to my family; we'd talk a lot afterward. • Making special gifts for friends. • Helping a discouraged classmate whose parents were going through a divorce.
COACHING/ TRAINING TEACHING • *Instructing*	• Teaching my cousin to ride a bike. • Playing softball; helping kids who were uncoordinated. • Going to summer camp; teaching kids to swim and do crafts. • Captain and leader of neighborhood games; really enjoyed the relationships. • Helping to teach a handicapped child after school.
COORDINATING OR FACILITATING • *Acting as PR rep or proponent* • *Sparking action*	• Putting together a three-mile bike trip for my friends; had a good time together. • Planning a surprise anniversary party for my parents. • Being chosen captain of safety patrol. • Catering and promoting a special party for a neighbor. • Representing our school at a convention. • Making the cheerleading team.

DISCOVER YOUR BEST POSSIBLE FUTURE

In looking over her Positive Experiences, Jennifer said to Tom, "I can see where some of my experiences fit. Most of them seem to fall under the Idea category. But I'm not sure of a few."

"Why don't you write them down where you think they fit, and put a question mark by the ones you're unsure of," Tom suggested.

Jennifer looked again at her Positive Experiences:

- Teaching myself to play organ.
- Being outdoors and exploring nature while camping with my family.
- Writing plays with my friend.
- Playing in a piano recital.
- Being on the debate team.
- Having my short story published in the school journal.
- Winning an award for an environmental contest and going to Boston to accept it from an important statesman.
- Taking advanced math and sciences.
- Playing piano accompaniment at church.
- Taking a long bike trip with the youth group.

Here's how she decided to categorize her Positive Experiences:

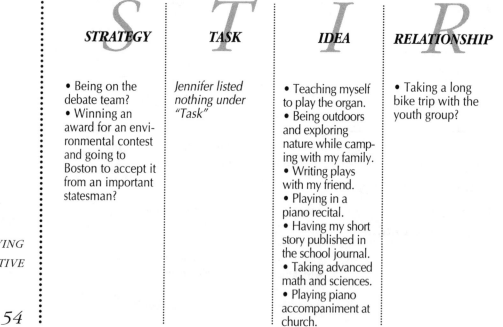

STRATEGY	**TASK**	**IDEA**	**RELATIONSHIP**
• Being on the debate team? • Winning an award for an environmental contest and going to Boston to accept it from an important statesman?	*Jennifer listed nothing under "Task"*	• Teaching myself to play the organ. • Being outdoors and exploring nature while camping with my family. • Writing plays with my friend. • Playing in a piano recital. • Having my short story published in the school journal. • Taking advanced math and sciences. • Playing piano accompaniment at church.	• Taking a long bike trip with the youth group?

"Most of my Positive Experiences fall into the Idea category," she said to Tom. "And I don't have a single thing under Task!"

"That's your Red area," Tom explained. "If Green is go, full-speed ahead, Red is stop. Not that you won't have to do the types of things listed under Task. You will. But you certainly don't want to pick a career that requires skills that are Red for you. And when you do have to do a Red, like typing, you can't expect yourself to perform at A or B level. If you do C-level work, you can feel OK about it. In your Green areas, you can expect to enjoy the work and do well at it—A or B level."

"I don't know, I never get C's, Tom. Maybe you're wrong," Jennifer said jokingly.

"Who types your papers?"

"I do," she said, "when I can't con my mom or big sister into doing it. And, you're right, I'm a terrible typist. I'm real slow. I'd hate being a secretary."

"That's because that is in the Task category, and Task is your Red." Tom eyed the pizza, which the waitress had just plunked down in front of them. "How about a break while we eat?" he suggested.

"Sure," she said. She ate a piece of pizza, wiped her fingers carefully, then looked thoughtfully at the list in front of her. "I'm still not sure about some of my Positive Experiences," she said. "Where does the debate team, or listening to music with a friend, fit in? What about my desire to make a difference, to help people? Debating seems to fit in the Strategy category, and helping people is Relationship."

Tom took a moment while he finished his first piece of pizza. "Most people will have a few things in other categories. Few people are pure Strategy, or Idea, or Relationship, or Task," he replied. "The things that show up less often are Yellow, rather than Green, to use the traffic light metaphor. Green means go, Yellow means proceed with caution. Your career will have, and should have, some amount of Yellow. But too much of it will

*Few people
are pure
Strategy, or
Idea, or
Relationship,
or Task. The
things that
show up less
often are
Yellow,
rather than
Green, to use
the traffic
light
metaphor.*

tend to turn it into a Red—something you won't do at a very high level. What we want to look for here is the thread that occurs most often. As you said, that seems to be Idea.

"What we can do is look at my notes from your Discovery Conversation," Tom continued. "I think when we find out exactly what you did and what you enjoyed, it will become clear which category you fall into. I just happen to have another list that will also help us with this. But please, can we finish the pizza first?"

While they ate, Jennifer's head spun. It was fascinating to her to see some patterns in her Positive Experiences, and encouraging to know it all meant something and would lead somewhere. Tom had said that God designed her with a purpose in mind, gave her gifts that she could find satisfaction in using. As she began to glimpse that design, she felt excitement rising in her.

"OK," Tom said, wiping his mouth, "let's look at what you said about the Positive Experiences you're not sure of. You said what you enjoyed about the debate team was the preparation— researching your subject, coming up with persuasive arguments. Let's turn to Step Two and see what that action skill falls under. Actually, you'll be able to pinpoint all your Green Action Skills if you go through each Positive Experience and check off what you did in each, using this chart I just happen to have. It's on the next page of the Self-assessment Guide."   Jennifer turned to the following page in the Self-assessment Guide.

"This should help with your questions," Tom said. "Write your Positive Experiences in the spaces provided across the top of the page. Then read the questions, and just put a check mark in the box that corresponds to what you did in each Positive Experience. If you can't remember what you did, we'll consult my notes from your Discovery Conversation."

Jennifer wrote her Positive Experiences in the spaces across the top of the page. She then went down the list of questions and marked the boxes that best described what she did in each Positive Experience. *This is what her chart looked like.*

Jennifer's Action Skills Assessment

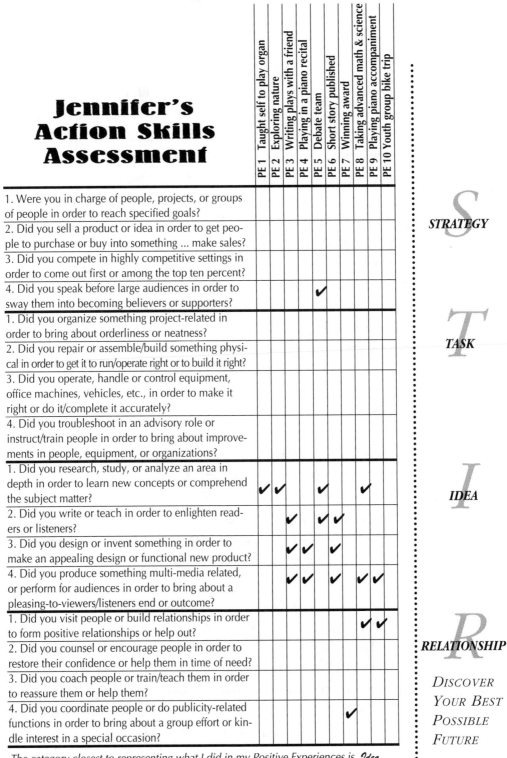

	PE 1 Taught self to play organ	PE 2 Exploring nature	PE 3 Writing plays with a friend	PE 4 Playing in a piano recital	PE 5 Debate team	PE 6 Short story published	PE 7 Winning award	PE 8 Taking advanced math & science	PE 9 Playing piano accompaniment	PE 10 Youth group bike trip	
STRATEGY											
1. Were you in charge of people, projects, or groups of people in order to reach specified goals?											
2. Did you sell a product or idea in order to get people to purchase or buy into something ... make sales?											
3. Did you compete in highly competitive settings in order to come out first or among the top ten percent?											
4. Did you speak before large audiences in order to sway them into becoming believers or supporters?				✔							
TASK											
1. Did you organize something project-related in order to bring about orderliness or neatness?											
2. Did you repair or assemble/build something physical in order to get it to run/operate right or to build it right?											
3. Did you operate, handle or control equipment, office machines, vehicles, etc., in order to make it right or do it/complete it accurately?											
4. Did you troubleshoot in an advisory role or instruct/train people in order to bring about improvements in people, equipment, or organizations?											
IDEA											
1. Did you research, study, or analyze an area in depth in order to learn new concepts or comprehend the subject matter?	✔	✔		✔				✔			
2. Did you write or teach in order to enlighten readers or listeners?			✔		✔	✔					
3. Did you design or invent something in order to make an appealing design or functional new product?			✔	✔		✔					
4. Did you produce something multi-media related, or perform for audiences in order to bring about a pleasing-to-viewers/listeners end or outcome?			✔	✔		✔		✔	✔		
RELATIONSHIP											
1. Did you visit people or build relationships in order to form positive relationships or help out?								✔	✔		
2. Did you counsel or encourage people in order to restore their confidence or help them in time of need?											
3. Did you coach people or train/teach them in order to reassure them or help them?											
4. Did you coordinate people or do publicity-related functions in order to bring about a group effort or kindle interest in a special occasion?							✔				

The category closest to representing what I did in my Positive Experiences is Idea
The category least representative of what I did in my Positive Experiences is Task

DISCOVER YOUR BEST POSSIBLE FUTURE

After Jennifer had marked her boxes, Tom said, "If you count up how many checks you have in each category, you'll have a list of all your Green Action Skills. The ones with the most check marks, of course, are your strongest skills. The ones with only a few marks are your Yellows. And of course, the skills you never checked at all are Red."

"I can see that I'm clearly in the Ideas category," Jennifer said, hunching over her chart. "Most of my Positive Experiences involved learning, writing, or performing musically. But I'm still not sure what to do about winning the award, or the bike trip with the youth group."

Tom pulled out yet another chart. "Remember the definition of a Positive Experience—something you enjoyed doing, something that gave you satisfaction? This next step in self-assessment should clear up any questions you still have, and will help you pinpoint just what you need in order for your work to be fulfilling to you."

He handed Jennifer another chart, similar to the first one. "Write your Positive Experiences across the top of the page, as you did in the previous chart," he instructed. "Then, think for a minute about two or three things about that positive experience that were satisfying to you. Go down the chart of questions and sample comments on satisfaction, and check the boxes that best describe what you enjoyed about the experience." Jennifer again jotted down her Positive Experiences across the top of the chart, and checked the boxes that matched what she remembered was satisfying about each experience.

"This is pretty easy," Jennifer said after she marked up the Satisfaction Assessment. "I can see that 'Being on the debate team' belongs more in Ideas, because what I enjoyed was the research and persuading others in order to enlighten them."

Tom said, "If you had said you enjoyed debate team in order to 'sell' people on your position and sway their thinking, you would have put that Positive Experience under Strategy. What did you do with 'winning the environmental award'?"

"I put that in Relationship, because what I did involved coordinating a group to work together, and what was satisfying was the recognition and the feeling that we made a difference in how others think about the environment. 'Taking a long bike trip with the youth group' stayed in Relationship, because building relationships was the highlight of that trip. Still, being outdoors was an important part of that experience, so I marked Idea also."

"Bravo!" Tom said with a big smile. "You've really caught on to this. But then, I'm not surprised—Ideas is your thing, right? No wonder you do so well in school."

Jennifer finished the last of her Pepsi with a big slurp. "So now I know I'm an Idea person, that I like to perform musically, write and learn. Does this mean I should be a musician?"

"That's one option," Tom replied. "It really depends on you. I suggest you don't rush into any decisions quite yet. Take this material, mull it over, and see if you still think it fits after you've lived with it a while. We'll get together another time to look at how this knowledge can influence decisions about your future. Maybe we'll try Mexican food next time?"

"Sounds good," Jennifer said, slipping out of the booth and grabbing her jacket. "But we can't wait too long. Those college applications are waiting, and I do have to make some decisions soon."

That night Jennifer showed her parents her Self-assessment Guide, and explained what she had learned about herself. "This tells me that I love to learn and I need to express what I'm learning in some form—writing or music or a debate or a project that will make a difference," she said with excitement. "I knew all these things about myself, in a way, but they weren't as focused as they are now."

"This looks really helpful," her mom said, eyeing the charts Jennifer had filled out. "Maybe I should take this assessment myself!"

If you count up how many checks you have in each category, you'll have a list of all your Green Action Skills.

Jennifer's Satisfaction Assessment

	PE 1 Taught self to play organ	PE 2 Exploring nature	PE 3 Writing plays with a friend	PE 4 Playing in a piano recital	PE 5 Debate team	PE 6 Short story published	PE 7 Winning award	PE 8 Taking advanced math & sciences	PE 9 Playing piano accompaniment	PE 10 Youth group bike trip
1. Did you need to win or surmount severe difficulties? WHAT I FOUND SATISFYING: *"Overcoming the obstacles, the competition, winning, pushing myself to the limit."*					✔			✔		
2. Were you at your best when in charge or in front of audiences? WHAT I FOUND SATISFYING: *"Being in front of large audiences ... being in charge, being totally responsible for whatever happened."*				✔						
3. Did you have to see immediate progress and results quickly? WHAT I FOUND SATISFYING: *"Noticing progress right away, seeing measurable results, knowing right away I was making the grade."*	✔									
1. Did you want to make it better or do it better/faster? WHAT I FOUND SATISFYING: *"Becoming proficient at it, doing it properly ... solving problems and making it right ... improving it."*										
2. Did you shape up or clean up an area, or correct flaws/errors? WHAT I FOUND SATISFYING: *"Getting it right, making it orderly ... it came out looking right—neat, polished, perfect."*										
3. Did you want to make decisions without relying a lot on others and do something right? WHAT I FOUND SATISFYING: *"Making my own decisions, being independent, no one interfered so it was done right."*										

S **STRATEGY**

T **TASK**

PLAYING DETECTIVE

60

Jennifer's Satisfaction Assessment

	PE 1 Taught self to play organ	PE 2 Exploring nature	PE 3 Writing plays with a friend	PE 4 Playing in a piano recital	PE 5 Debate team	PE 6 Short story published	PE 7 Winning award	PE 8 Taking advanced math & sciences	PE 9 Playing piano accompaniment	PE 10 Youth group bike trip
1. Did you seek to acquire knowledge, expertise, comprehension? WHAT I FOUND SATISFYING: *"Feeling like I was on a treasure hunt and discovering new truths, facts ... the learning and understanding of it ... becoming engrossed in the process."*	✔	✔		✔		✔	✔		✔	
2. Did you want to make or form a visible or audible end-product/end-expression? WHAT I FOUND SATISFYING: *"The creative process, seeing it go from nothing to something ... expressing myself ... making, producing beauty and harmony."*	✔		✔	✔		✔			✔	
1. Did you like being appreciated, affirmed? WHAT I FOUND SATISFYING: *"Their approval and compliments ... their immediate acceptance ... noticing their change, frowns changing to smiles."*					✔	✔	✔			
2. Did you enjoy doing things with others, helping out? WHAT I FOUND SATISFYING: *"Doing it together, the camaraderie ... developing relationships, simply helping people ... that everyone pitched in ... being part of a cooperative effort."*			✔						✔	✔
3. Did you like to be special to someone and/or do something different, distinctive? WHAT I FOUND SATISFYING: *"It was unique, one of a kind ... doing something others normally do not do ... it was new and different ... being their special helper or confidant."*							✔			

I **IDEA**

R **RELATIONSHIP**

DISCOVER YOUR BEST POSSIBLE FUTURE

"Go ahead, Mom," Jennifer urged. "It's simple. I can even show you how to interpret it. You have to start by listing your Positive Experiences...."

We'll come back to Jennifer in the next chapter. But to give you another example of how to assess your Positive Experiences, let's work through the process once more with Jeff.

Jeff Finds New Direction

Remember Jeff from Chapter Two? We've already listened in on his Discovery Conversation with Mrs. Hartwell, in which he described in detail his first three Positive Experiences. After talking about what gave him fulfillment, he felt a strange combination of pleasure—from recounting the things he did he felt good about—and pain—because the things he felt best about were connected to sports. It was a reminder that sports was out of the picture for him now that he had a bum knee.

Mrs. Hartwell had taken notes and taped Jeff's Discovery Conversation. She gave Jeff the notes and tape, along with the Self-assessment Guide. "Sit down with this and fill it out, then come back and we'll talk about it," she had suggested. Now, as Jeff sat in his room with his pencil in hand, he wondered if all this work would really help him. The deadlines for applying to colleges loomed.

With his Positive Experiences List in hand, along with Mrs. Hartwell's notes from his Discovery Conversation, he opened up the Self-assessment Guide to Step One. He added his Positive Experiences under the categories where they seemed to fit best. Jeff wasn't sure where to put "serving as president of a regional high-school church conference," and "voted 'best actor,' " so he left them in two of the S-T-I-R categories. Mrs. Hartwell had suggested that, if he came upon questions, he should just continue the process. "Often your questions will be answered by the time you finish Step Three," she had explained. "If they aren't, feel free to come see me."

So Jeff turned to Step Two and wrote each of his Positive Experiences across the top of the chart. Then he checked the boxes that seemed to fit what he did in each Positive Experience. At times he glanced at the notes from his Discovery Conversation.

Step Three instructed him to focus on what was satisfying about his Positive Experiences. But before filling out the Satisfaction Assessment, he glanced at the notes Mrs. Hartwell had taken when they did the Discovery Conversation. He highlighted the quotes of what he had said about what satisfied him in each experience. Here's what he highlighted:

Period 1: Ages 5-12

Hitting a home run in Little League. *"It was the kind of hit they made in the big leagues."*

Became popular and a leader in our neighborhood, even though we had just moved to a new area. *"Going from the new kid nobody knew to being the one everyone looked up to. Coming up with new ideas and being in charge. Playing sports."*

Admitted to Order of the Arrow, a special group within Boy Scouts. *"Being chosen, someone special ... I was one of the best. I felt privileged."*

Winning student council election. *"People thought I was the best person to do the job. Just winning was a thrill."*

In sixth-grade gym class, my team never lost. *"Winning, the feeling that together we were unbeatable."*

Period 2: Ages 13-18

Voted "best actor" in sophomore English class. *"I liked being in front of people, acting, and I liked that they thought I was so good."*

Getting on the football team and playing varsity. *"Making the team as a junior—few people did ... the thrill of the game, the competition ... winning ... pushing myself to my physical limits."*

Selling candy to raise money for our youth group. *"Getting people to buy the candy, and selling more than anyone else."*

Serving as president of a regional high-school church conference. *"Being in charge, having people come to me with questions or problems ... getting to know new people, and helping them to work together on projects."*

Working on the school yearbook. *"Making sure things got done ... working with others and meeting new people."*

Sample Assessment Guide
with Jeff's Comments

GREEN ACTION SKILLS	SAMPLE POSITIVE EXPERIENCES	JEFF'S POSITIVE EXPERIENCES
DIRECTING • *Being in charge* • *Running the show*	• Setting up Kool-Aid stands around town manned by people I recruited. • Starting a neighborhood newspaper; recruiting writers and salespeople. • Planning and developing the largest garden in the county. • Heading up a group of majorettes in grade school. • Tripling the size of my paper route; hiring friends to help. • Directing and organizing kids to build a tree fort; duplicating it for a school-mate in another neighborhood.	*Became popular and the leader in our neighborhood, even though we had just moved to a new area* *Serving as president of a regional high School*
PERSUADING • *Selling* • *Promoting* • *Recruiting* • *Debating* • *Negotiating*	• Selling the most Girl Scout cookies; setting a record. • Campaigning for ____ when he ran for president. • Selling soft drinks at a circus. • Selling advertising for a local newspaper. • Winning a recruiting contest. • Promoting and selling a classmate singer to teachers and businesses.	*Selling candy to raise money for our youth group (I sold the most).* *Winning student council election in fourth grade.*
SPEAKING	• Giving speeches in class. • Emceeing for a talent show. • Winning the Optimist speech contest. • Giving pep talks to neighborhood kids.	*Winning student council election in fourth grade. (I gave lots of speeches).*
COMPETING • *Outdoing* • *Outmaneuvering* • *Outthinking*	• Playing soccer against stiff competition. • Racing go-carts. • Doing well against adults in Monopoly, chess, and card games. • Out-strategizing opponents in wrestling and tennis. • Competing on a ski team. • Winning debates.	*Hitting a home run in little league.* *Admitted to the order of the arrow in Boy Scouts.* *Sixth-grade gym class—my team never lost.* *Voted Best Actor in sophomore English class* *Getting on the football team and playing varsity.*

GREEN ACTION SKILLS	SAMPLE POSITIVE EXPERIENCES	JEFF'S POSITIVE EXPERIENCES
STRAIGHTENING OUT/ORGANIZING • *Setting up* • *Arranging* • *Cleaning*	• Helping at home doing vacuuming and cleaning. • Setting up a movie theater in our garage. • Keeping my room neat, clean, and organized. • Head dishwasher at camp. • Keeping the garden weed-free; shoveling snow off sidewalks. • Stacking hay bales neatly ... they never fell down.	
OPERATING/HANDLING OR CONTROLLING • *Tools, equipment, vehicles* • *At a keyboard or controls*	• Learning to play a pump organ by myself. • School projectionist; training others to operate it. • Teaching myself to type. • Teaching archery at a camp. • Perfected cursive writing skills. • Operating farm equipment for a neighbor. • Learning to ride and control my bike; could follow a line precisely while riding.	
REPAIRING OR ASSEMBLING/BUILDING • *Fixing* • *Constructing*	• Building models from kits. • Installing stereo equipment throughout our house. • Building a garage with blocks; was intricately put together. • Fixing clocks. • Making scaled-down furniture. • Building campfires. • Repairing toys for friends. • Doing small household repairs. • Repairing my grandmother's toaster.	
TROUBLESHOOTING OR INSTRUCTING • *Advising* • *Teaching*	• Teaching archery at a camp. • Finding out why my camera didn't work right. • Being an "adviser" to a substitute teacher. • Helping my brother figure out how to operate his computer. • Teaching my dog several tricks. • Problem-solving with kids having difficulty with school work.	*Working on the school yearbook*

GREEN ACTION SKILLS	SAMPLE POSITIVE EXPERIENCES	JEFF'S POSITIVE EXPERIENCES
RESEARCHING • *Studying* • *Exploring* • *Investigating*	• Reading voraciously. • Studying history, biographies ... can get "lost" in them. • Doing math, coming up with math theories. • Studying astronomy. • Taking trips to the library. • Learning math from my mother. • Researching solar energy; doing a science project on weather. • Hiking, exploring lakes, caves ... studying the forest, birds, flowers. • Being outdoors, discovering things in nature. • Visiting historical places; taking time to think and reflect.	
WRITING OR TEACHING • *Instructing* • *Tutoring*	• Writing well in English class. • Writing a novel and short story on my own. • Working on the school newspaper. • Writing and illustrating a booklet about dogs. • Playing school; I was always the teacher. • Helping my brother learn arithmetic.	
CREATING/SHAPING/ EXPRESSING • *Performing* • *Making* • *Designing* • *Inventing*	• Acting out songs I created and wrote. • Drawing and painting landscape scenes. • Sculpturing in art class. • Playing piano ... a way to express myself. • Building a crude digital computer for a science fair.	*Voted Best Actor in sophomore English class*

GREEN ACTION SKILLS	SAMPLE POSITIVE EXPERIENCES	JEFF'S POSITIVE EXPERIENCES
VISITING OR BUILDING RELATIONSHIPS • *Befriending* • *Helping*	• Traveling to various parts of the country and meeting different kinds of people. • Being a volunteer Candy Striper. • Visiting people while selling cookies. • Playing softball; made a lot of friends. • Being close to my grandparents. • Making friends on my paper route. • Going to camp to meet new people.	
COUNSELING OR ENCOURAGING • *Waiting on* • *Helping*	• Talking to friends, listening to their problems. • Counseling crippled children at camps. • Visiting the elderly at a nursing home. • Helping a sickly aunt; I mainly listened. • Making and serving desserts to my family; we'd talk a lot afterward. • Making special gifts for friends. • Helping a discouraged classmate whose parents were going through a divorce.	
COACHING/ TRAINING TEACHING • *Instructing*	• Teaching my cousin to ride a bike. • Playing softball; helping kids who were uncoordinated. • Going to summer camp; teaching kids to swim and do crafts. • Captain and leader of neighborhood games; really enjoyed the relationships. • Helping to teach a handicapped child after school.	
COORDINATING OR FACILITATING • *Acting as PR rep or proponent* • *Sparking action*	• Putting together a three-mile bike trip for my friends; had a good time together. • Planning a surprise anniversary party for my parents. • Being chosen captain of safety patrol. • Catering and promoting a special party for a neighbor. • Representing our school at a convention. • Making the cheerleading team.	*Serving as president of a regional high school church conference.*

DISCOVER YOUR BEST POSSIBLE FUTURE

By looking at where his check marks clustered on the Satisfaction Assessment, Jeff saw pretty clearly that Strategy was the category that fit most of his Positive Experiences. But he wasn't sure what that meant. It heartened him to see that sports had never totally been his whole life; there were other kinds of Positive Experiences that, according to Mrs. Hartwell, could lead to satisfying work. He decided to make an appointment with Mrs. Hartwell to discuss what being a "Strategy" person meant for his future.

The next day at school he stopped by Mrs. Hartwell's office to see if she had any free time.

"Mrs. Hartwell?"

She looked up from some papers she was studying at her desk.

"Oh, hi, Jeff. What can I do for you?" *(Continued on page 70.)*

Jeff's Action Skills Assessment

	PE 1 Hitting a home run	PE 2 Became a leader in neighborhood	PE 3 Admitted to special Boy Scout group	PE 4 Won student council election	PE 5 Team never lost in 6th grade	PE 6 Voted 'best actor'	PE 7 Playing varsity football	PE 8 Selling candy for fundraiser	PE 9 President of church conference	PE 10 School yearbook
1. Were you in charge of people, projects, or groups of people in order to reach specified goals?	✔	✔							✔	✔
2. Did you sell a product or idea in order to get people to purchase or buy into something ... make sales?			✔					✔		
3. Did you compete in highly competitive settings in order to come out first or among the top ten percent?	✔	✔	✔	✔	✔	✔				
4. Did you speak before large audiences in order to sway them into becoming believers or supporters?				✔						

STRATEGY

68

Jeff's Action Skills Assessment

	PE 1 Hitting a home run	PE 2 Became a leader in neighborhood	PE 3 Admitted to special Boy Scout group	PE 4 Won student council election	PE 5 Team never lost in 6th grade	PE 6 Voted 'best actor'	PE 7 Playing varsity football	PE 8 Selling candy for fundraiser	PE 9 President of church conference	PE 10 School yearbook	
1. Did you organize something project-related in order to bring about orderliness or neatness?											
2. Did you repair or assemble/build something physical in order to get it to run/operate right or to build it right?											*T* TASK
3. Did you operate, handle or control equipment, office machines, vehicles, etc., in order to make it right or do it/complete it accurately?											
4. Did you troubleshoot in an advisory role or instruct/train people in order to bring about improvements in people, equipment or organizations?									✔		
1. Did you research, study or analyze an area in depth in order to learn new concepts or comprehend the subject matter?											
2. Did you write or teach in order to enlighten readers or listeners?											*I* IDEA
3. Did you design or invent something in order to make an appealing design or functional new product?											
4. Did you produce something multi-media related, or perform for audiences in order to bring about a pleasing-to-viewers/listeners end or outcome?						✔					
1. Did you visit people or build relationships in order to form positive relationships or help out?	✔	✔									
2. Did you counsel or encourage people in order to restore their confidence or help them in time of need?									✔		*R* RELATIONSHIP
3. Did you coach people or train/teach them in order to reassure them or help them?								✔	✔		
4. Did you coordinate people or do publicity-related functions in order to bring about a group effort or kindle interest in a special occasion?							✔		✔	✔	

*The category closest to representing what I did in my Positive Experiences is ... **Strategy.***
*The category least representative of what I did in my Positive Experiences is ...**Task.***

69

Jeff said, "Well, I finished the self-assessment, and I'm wondering now just what it all means. Can I make an appointment?"

"If you're free this period, I have a cancellation," she said.

"As a matter of fact, this is a study hall for me, so that would work," he said. He put his books down and rummaged around his notebook for his Self-assessment Guide. "Found it," he muttered. "OK, from all this it's pretty clear that I'm a 'Strategy' person. But what does that mean?"

"Let's have a look," Mrs. Hartwell said. After studying his Guide for a moment, she said, "Well, it seems to me that this tells you what you do best—compete, direct, coordinate, even speak before audiences or sell. Also it tells us what gives you satisfaction— winning, overcoming difficulties, being in charge, and being special. You tell me, what kind of career comes to mind that might use these qualities?"

"Maybe I should go into business," he said. Excitement grew in him like a storm brewing. A dim picture of a successful executive started to form in the back of his mind.

"Maybe you should," Mrs. Hartwell agreed. "From what you have here, it would appear to be a pretty good fit."

"What's my next step, counselor?" Jeff asked with a grin.

"Well, it seems to me you said you have some college applications to fill out. Why don't you check into some schools that have a good business program, but also a strong liberal arts reputation. That way you'll leave lots of options open. Remember, you don't have to set your future in concrete yet."

"This has been real helpful. Thanks a lot, Mrs. Hartwell. I'm really beginning to feel better about my future," Jeff told her as he got up.

"You should," she replied. "You have a lot going for you."

"Thanks again." As Jeff strode down the hallway to his locker, he felt great. So what if he had a bum knee—there were other things he could do, and do well. For the first time in over a year, his future began to look rosy again.

Jeff's Satisfaction Assessment

	PE 1 Hitting a home run	PE 2 Became a leader in neighborhood	PE 3 Admitted to special Boy Scout group	PE 4 Won student council election	PE 5 Team never lost in 6th grade	PE 6 Voted 'best actor'	PE 7 Playing varsity (football)	PE 8 Selling candy for fundraiser	PE 9 President of church conference	PE 10 School yearbook
1. Did you need to win or surmount severe difficulties? WHAT I FOUND SATISFYING: *"Overcoming the obstacles, the competition, winning, pushing myself to the limit."*	✔		✔	✔	✔		✔			
2. Were you at your best when in charge or in front of audiences? WHAT I FOUND SATISFYING: *"Being in front of large audiences ... being in charge, being totally responsible for whatever happened."*		✔		✔		✔			✔	✔
3. Did you have to see immediate progress and results quickly? WHAT I FOUND SATISFYING: *"Noticing progress right away, seeing measurable results, knowing right away I was making the grade."*	✔						✔	✔		
1. Did you want to make it better or do it better/faster? WHAT I FOUND SATISFYING: *"Becoming proficient at it, doing it properly ... solving problems and making it right ... improving it."*										
2. Did you shape up or clean up an area, or correct flaws/errors? WHAT I FOUND SATISFYING: *"Getting it right, making it orderly... it came out looking right—neat, polished, perfect."*										
3. Did you want to make decisions without relying a lot on others and do something right? WHAT I FOUND SATISFYING: *"Making my own decisions, being independent, no one interfered so it was done right."*										

S STRATEGY

T TASK

DISCOVER YOUR BEST POSSIBLE FUTURE

Jeff's Satisfaction Assessment

	PE 1 Hitting a home run	PE 2 Became a leader in neighborhood	PE 3 Admitted to special Boy Scout group	PE 4 Won student council election	PE 5 Team never lost in 6th grade	PE 6 Voted 'best actor'	PE 7 Playing varsity football	PE 8 Selling candy for fundraiser	PE 9 President of church conference	PE 10 School yearbook
IDEA 1. Did you seek to acquire knowledge, expertise, comprehension? WHAT I FOUND SATISFYING: *"Feeling like I was on a treasure hunt and discovering new truths, facts... the learning and understanding of it ... becoming engrossed in the process."*			✔							
2. Did you want to make or form a visible or audible end product/end expression? WHAT I FOUND SATISFYING: *"The creative process, seeing it go from nothing to something... expressing myself... making, producing beauty and harmony."*						✔				✔
RELATIONSHIP 1. Did you like being appreciated, affirmed? WHAT I FOUND SATISFYING: *"Their approval and compliments ... their immediate acceptance ... noticing their change, frowns changing to smiles."*		✔	✔		✔					
2. Did you enjoy doing things with others, helping out? WHAT I FOUND SATISFYING: *"Doing it together, the camaraderie ... developing relationships, simply helping people ... that everyone pitched in ... being part of a cooperative effort."*									✔	✔
PLAYING DETECTIVE 3. Did you like to be special to someone and/or do something different, destinctive? WHAT I FOUND SATISFYING: *"It was unique, one of a kind ... doing something others normally do not do ... it was new and different ... being their special helper or confidant."*		✔	✔	✔					✔	✔

IDEA

RELATIONSHIP

PLAYING DETECTIVE

We'll come back to Jeff later to find out how this new knowledge will help him choose a college and a direction. Now it's your turn.

CHAPTER 4

Discover Your Green Action Skills

YOU'VE SEEN HOW JENNIFER AND JEFF INTERPRETED their Positive Experiences. Let's go through each step one more time. This time we urge you to fill in the forms with your own responses. (Turn the page for the full format.)

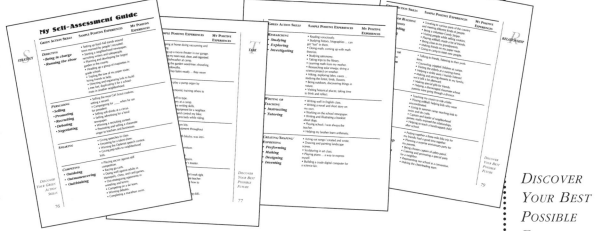

STEP ONE. Compare your list of Positive Experiences to the sample PEs on the following pages. Add yours wherever they seem to fit best.

DISCOVER YOUR BEST POSSIBLE FUTURE

My Self-Assessment Guide

GREEN ACTION SKILLS	SAMPLE POSITIVE EXPERIENCES	MY POSITIVE EXPERIENCES
DIRECTING • *Being in charge* • *Running the show*	• Setting up Kool-Aid stands around town manned by people I recruited. • Starting a neighborhood newspaper; recruiting writers and salespeople. • Planning and developing the largest garden in the county. • Heading up a group of majorettes in grade school. • Tripling the size of my paper route; hiring friends to help. • Directing and organizing kids to build a tree fort; duplicating it for a schoolmate in another neighborhood.	
PERSUADING • *Selling* • *Promoting* • *Recruiting* • *Debating* • *Negotiating*	• Selling the most Girl Scout cookies; setting a record. • Campaigning for ____ when he ran for president. • Selling soft drinks at a circus. • Selling advertising for a local newspaper. • Winning a recruiting contest. • Promoting and selling a classmate singer to teachers and businesses.	
SPEAKING	• Giving speeches in class. • Emceeing for a talent show. • Winning the Optimist speech contest. • Giving pep talks to neighborhood kids.	
COMPETING • *Outdoing* • *Outmaneuvering* • *Outthinking*	• Playing soccer against stiff competition. • Racing go-carts. • Doing well against adults in Monopoly, chess, and card games. • Out-strategizing opponents in wrestling and tennis. • Competing on a ski team. • Winning debates. • Completing a marathon swim.	

GREEN ACTION SKILLS	SAMPLE POSITIVE EXPERIENCES	MY POSITIVE EXPERIENCES
STRAIGHTENING OUT/ORGANIZING • *Setting up* • *Arranging* • *Cleaning*	• Helping at home doing vacuuming and cleaning. • Setting up a movie theater in our garage. • Keeping my room neat, clean, and organized. • Head dishwasher at camp. • Keeping the garden weed-free; shoveling snow off sidewalks. • Stacking hay bales neatly ... they never fell down.	
OPERATING/HANDLING OR CONTROLLING • *Tools, equipment, vehicles* • *At a keyboard or controls*	• Learning to play a pump organ by myself. • School projectionist; training others to operate it. • Teaching myself to type. • Teaching archery at a camp. • Perfected cursive writing skills. • Operating farm equipment for a neighbor. • Learning to ride and control my bike; could follow a line precisely while riding.	
REPAIRING OR ASSEMBLING/BUILDING • *Fixing* • *Constructing*	• Building models from kits. • Installing stereo equipment throughout our house. • Building a garage with blocks; was intricately put together. • Fixing clocks. • Making scaled-down furniture. • Building campfires. • Repairing toys for friends. • Doing small household repairs. • Repairing my grandmother's toaster.	
TROUBLESHOOTING OR INSTRUCTING • *Advising* • *Teaching*	• Teaching archery at a camp. • Finding out why my camera didn't work right. • Being an "adviser" to a substitute teacher. • Helping my brother figure out how to operate his computer. • Teaching my dog several tricks. • Problem-solving with kids having difficulty with school work.	

DISCOVER YOUR BEST POSSIBLE FUTURE

GREEN ACTION SKILLS	SAMPLE POSITIVE EXPERIENCES	MY POSITIVE EXPERIENCES
RESEARCHING • *Studying* • *Exploring* • *Investigating*	• Reading voraciously. • Studying history, biographies ... can get "lost" in them. • Doing math, coming up with math theories. • Studying astronomy. • Taking trips to the library. • Learning math from my mother. • Researching solar energy; doing a science project on weather. • Hiking, exploring lakes, caves ... studying the forest, birds, flowers. • Being outdoors, discovering things in nature. • Visiting historical places; taking time to think and reflect.	
WRITING OR TEACHING • *Instructing* • *Tutoring*	• Writing well in English class. • Writing a novel and short story on my own. • Working on the school newspaper. • Writing and illustrating a booklet about dogs. • Playing school; I was always the teacher. • Helping my brother learn arithmetic.	
CREATING/SHAPING/ EXPRESSING • *Performing* • *Making* • *Designing* • *Inventing*	• Acting out songs I created and wrote. • Drawing and painting landscape scenes. • Sculpturing in art class. • Playing piano ... a way to express myself. • Building a crude digital computer for a science fair.	

GREEN ACTION SKILLS	SAMPLE POSITIVE EXPERIENCES	MY POSITIVE EXPERIENCES
VISITING OR BUILDING RELATIONSHIPS • *Befriending* • *Helping*	• Traveling to various parts of the country and meeting different kinds of people. • Being a volunteer Candy Striper. • Visiting people while selling cookies. • Playing softball; made a lot of friends. • Being close to my grandparents. • Making friends on my paper route. • Going to camp to meet new people.	
COUNSELING OR ENCOURAGING • *Waiting on* • *Helping*	• Talking to friends, listening to their problems. • Counseling crippled children at camps. • Visiting the elderly at a nursing home. • Helping a sickly aunt; I mainly listened. • Making and serving desserts to my family; we'd talk a lot afterward. • Making special gifts for friends. • Helping a discouraged classmate whose parents were going through a divorce.	
COACHING/ TRAINING TEACHING • *Instructing*	• Teaching my cousin to ride a bike. • Playing softball; helping kids who were uncoordinated. • Going to summer camp; teaching kids to swim and do crafts. • Captain and leader of neighborhood games; really enjoyed the relationships. • Helping to teach a handicapped child after school.	
COORDINATING OR FACILITATING • *Acting as PR rep or proponent* • *Sparking action*	• Putting together a three-mile bike trip for my friends; had a good time together. • Planning a surprise anniversary party for my parents. • Being chosen captain of safety patrol. • Catering and promoting a special party for a neighbor. • Representing our school at a convention. • Making the cheerleading team.	

RELATIONSHIP

DISCOVER YOUR BEST POSSIBLE FUTURE

STEP TWO. Write down your Positive Experiences in the spaces provided at the top of the chart below. Think of two or three things you did in each one. Read the following questions, and put a check mark or X in the box that describes what you did in each Positive Experience.

STRATEGY

DISCOVER
YOUR
GREEN
ACTION
SKILLS

80

My Action Skills
Assessment

	PE 1	PE 2	PE 3	PE 4	PE 5	PE 6	PE 7	PE 8	PE 9	PE 10
1. Were you in charge of people, projects, or groups of people in order to reach specified goals?										
2. Did you sell a product or idea in order to get people to purchase or buy into something ... make sales?										
3. Did you compete in highly competitive settings in order to come out first or among the top ten percent?										
4. Did you speak before large audiences in order to sway them into becoming believers or supporters?										

My Action Skills Assessment

	PE 1	PE 2	PE 3	PE 4	PE 5	PE 6	PE 7	PE 8	PE 9	PE 10
1. Did you organize something project-related in order to bring about orderliness or neatness?										
2. Did you repair or assemble/build something physical in order to get it to run/operate right or to build it right?										
3. Did you operate, handle, or control equipment, office machines, vehicles, etc., in order to make it right or do it/complete it accurately?										
4. Did you troubleshoot in an advisory role or instruct/train people in order to bring about improvements in people, equipment, or organizations?										
1. Did you research, study, or analyze an area in depth in order to learn new concepts or comprehend the subject matter?										
2. Did you write or teach in order to enlighten readers or listeners?										
3. Did you design or invent something in order to make an appealing design or functional new product?										
4. Did you produce something multi-media related, or perform for audiences in order to bring about a pleasing-to-viewers/listeners end or outcome?										
1. Did you visit people or build relationships in order to form positive relationships or help out?										
2. Did you counsel or encourage people in order to restore their confidence or help them in time of need?										
3. Did you coach people or train/teach them in order to reassure them or help them?										
4. Did you coordinate people or do publicity-related functions in order to bring about a group effort or kindle interest in a special occasion?										

T TASK

I IDEA

R RELATIONSHIP

DISCOVER YOUR BEST POSSIBLE

The category closest to representing what I did in my Positive Experiences is ....
The category least representative of what I did in my Positive Experiences is ....

STEP THREE. Now focus on what gave you satisfaction in each Positive Experience. Refer to your notes from your Discovery Conversation if you need to.

As you did in Step Two, write your Positive Experiences in the spaces across the top of the chart. Read the following examples of what people say about a Positive Experience when asked: "What was satisfying (or fulfilling) to you about that Positive Experience?" Then mark the boxes that come closest to describing what gave you satisfaction in each of your Positive Experiences.

Use this guide to double-check the category that fits you best, based on what was fulfilling about your Positive Experiences.

My Satisfaction Assessment

	PE 1	PE 2	PE 3	PE 4	PE 5	PE 6	PE 7	PE 8	PE 9	PE 10
1. Did you need to win or surmount severe difficulties? WHAT I FOUND SATISFYING: *"Overcoming the obstacles, the competition, winning, pushing myself to the limit."*										
2. Were you at your best when in charge or in front of audiences? WHAT I FOUND SATISFYING: *"Being in front of large audiences ... being in charge, being totally responsible for whatever happened."*										
3. Did you have to see immediate progress and results quickly? WHAT I FOUND SATISFYING: *"Noticing progress right away, seeing measurable results, knowing right away I was making the grade."*										
1. Did you want to make it better or do it better/faster? WHAT I FOUND SATISFYING: *"Becoming proficient at it, doing it properly ... solving problems and making it right ... improving it."*										
2. Did you shape up or clean up an area, or correct flaws/errors? WHAT I FOUND SATISFYING: *"Getting it right, making it orderly ... it came out looking right—neat, polished, perfect."*										
3. Did you want to make decisions without relying a lot on others and to do something right? WHAT I FOUND SATISFYING: *"Making my own decisions, being independent, no one interfered so it was done right."*										

S **STRATEGY**

T **TASK**

DISCOVER YOUR BEST POSSIBLE FUTURE

My Satisfaction Assessment

	PE 1	PE 2	PE 3	PE 4	PE 5	PE 6	PE 7	PE 8	PE 9	PE 10
1. Did you seek to acquire knowledge, expertise, comprehension? WHAT I FOUND SATISFYING: *"Feeling like I was on a treasure hunt and discovering new truths, facts ... the learning and understanding of it ... becoming engrossed in the process."*										
2. Did you want to make or form a visible or audible end product/end expression? WHAT I FOUND SATISFYING: *"The creative process, seeing it go from nothing to something ... expressing myself ... making, producing beauty and harmony."*										
1. Did you like being appreciated, affirmed? WHAT I FOUND SATISFYING: *"Their approval and compliments ... their immediate acceptance ... noticing their change, frowns changing to smiles."*										
2. Did you enjoy doing things with others, helping out? WHAT I FOUND SATISFYING: *"Doing it together, the camaraderie ... developing relationships, simply helping people ... that everyone pitched in ... being part of a cooperative effort."*										
3. Did you like to be special to someone and/or do something different, distinctive? WHAT I FOUND SATISFYING: *"It was unique, one of a kind ... doing something others normally do not do ... it was new and different ... being their special helper or confidant."*										

IDEA

RELATIONSHIP

DISCOVER
YOUR
GREEN
ACTION
SKILLS

84

STEP FOUR. Congratulate yourself! You've now done the hardest work—and wasn't it fun? You should now have a very clear idea whether your Green is Strategy, Task, Idea, or Relationship.

Just for fun, you might want to double-check what you've discovered against the following list of characteristics for each S-T-I-R category. You'll find some don't fit from your category, but many will. Circle the ones that do describe you, if you like. It will add to the picture of yourself and your strengths that is coming into focus, and may help you as you make decisions, such as which kind of college to attend.

Characteristics of the S-T-I-R Categories

STRATEGY

- Prefers to look at the big picture
- Hates details
- Dislikes puzzles and board games
- Takes advantage of opportunities
- Can be persuasive
- Likes to promote causes, ideas, people
- Is a crusader
- Likes a contest
- Feasts on mental combat, debating, outdoing
- Enjoys risk or danger
- May be described by others as a mover and shaker
- Relishes speed, doing things fast

T
TASK

- Easily and quickly settles into a pattern or routine
- Checks things twice
- Others describe as consistent, cautious, careful
- Does tasks by the book
- Follows written or mental checklists
- Tends to save money and be budget conscious
- Is bothered when there's a flaw in anything
  (for example, will straighten a crooked picture)
- Likes functioning independently
- Tends to be a "fixer-upper"
- Is safety conscious
- May like high-school math, but not advanced math
  (for example, differential equations)

I
IDEA

- Loves to learn new things
- Enjoys complex subjects
- Seeks beauty, balance, blending together
- Becomes engrossed, immersed in task at hand
- Gravitates to libraries, museums
- Hates board games
- Likes to read
- Enjoys words
- Appreciates the aesthetic
- Seeks ways to express ideas (designing, composing, writing, etc.)
- Is fascinated by different cultures
- Savors nature, environment, outdoors

- Relishes philosophy, arts, advanced math
- Likes to work with imagery, symbolism
- Needs solitude

*R*ELATIONSHIP

- Enjoys lending a helping hand
- May be involved in social service organizations, such as Big Brothers or Big Sisters
- Likes being outdoors
- Affirms others
- Values cooperative efforts
- Described by others as a "people person"
- Loves board games
- Enjoys serving others
- Savors special occasions
- Is drawn to sociology, psychology
- Likes volunteer work
- Needs recreational activities
- Prefers spontaneity, schedule flexibility rather than rigid routines
- Hates advanced math
- Relishes travel

A Clearer Picture of You-in Green!

Let's review what you now know about yourself.

You know whether your Green is Strategy, Task, Idea, or Relationship. More specifically, you can pinpoint what your Green Action Skills are—the GAS that will fuel you as you move ahead toward your future. These are the action skills you first pinpointed from your Positive Experiences in Step Two. You

Because of what you now know about yourself, many of the decisions you face will be easier.

know the kinds of conditions that give you satisfaction from Step Three. And you have some idea of your personal characteristics from Step Four.

Knowing these things, many of the decisions you face will become much easier, because you'll be working with facts about how God put you together rather than guesses about what you might enjoy.

In the next chapter we'll look at how all this can help you make decisions about what to do after high school.

Choosing Your Direction

RYAN WAS EXCITED. HE HAD MET WITH Dick Hagstrom, described his Positive Experiences, and worked through the Self-assessment Guide described in the last chapter. Ryan had discovered that his Green was Tasks, his Red Ideas. "That's why academic subjects have always been a struggle for you," Mr. Hagstrom explained. "You need to be working hands-on with what you're learning, and you need to see a clear reason for studying a subject." But building things, fixing things up— these showed up again and again in his Positive Experiences. Now Ryan faced his father with some concrete information and hope in his heart.

They sat down at the round dining room table, and Ryan showed his dad what he had learned.

"See, Dad, what I really like to do is build things or fix things up. Mr. Hagstrom says there's lots of careers I can do that in."

"OK, so what are you thinking about looking into?" his father asked. He was glad Ryan had taken the initiative to see Mr. Hagstrom, proud that his son had gone through the steps required to work through the Positive Experiences. He was see-

DISCOVER YOUR BEST POSSIBLE FUTURE

ing Ryan change from an unmotivated, uncommunicative person into someone who was beginning to glimpse a sense of purpose for his life.

"Well, I talked to a mechanic at the career fair who said he might hire someone to work for him. Maybe I can contact him and see if he has a job opening." Ryan could picture it now: Get a job right away, work and save money, gain experience, maybe even someday open his own shop.

"So you're thinking of getting a job right after graduation? What about going on to school?"

"You mean, like college?" The very thought of more school depressed Ryan. Though he'd taken college prep courses because his father had always assumed he'd go on to college, his SATs were low and his grades were terrible—mostly C's, even a few D's. What college would accept him?

"Maybe not," his father said. "But I was just reading in the newspaper the other day about jobs in the trades. It seems that most jobs like the kind you're talking about require more education. Mechanics use computers nowadays to diagnose car problems, and it seems they require more training than just a high-school education."

Ryan remembered what the mechanic at the careers fair had said. "Come to think of it, that's what the mechanic I talked to told me. He said something about training programs run by car manufacturers, and I think he also said the community college offers courses."

His father got up. "The catalog for the community college just came in the mail the other day. Let's take a look." He left the room to find the catalog.

Maybe school won't be so bad if it's in an area I'm interested in, Ryan mused. *I did like shop and did well in that. Maybe if I could take more courses like that, instead of English and history, I'd do OK.*

His dad returned with the catalog. It looked like a newspaper.

He opened it up to where it said "Automotive Service Technology" in bold print. "Looks like they have something here," he said. "Take a look." He handed Ryan the catalog.

Ryan scanned the courses with their cryptic abbreviations. "Engine Des & Opr"; "Electrical I"; "Auto Fuels I"; "Braking Systems"; "Sus Steer & Align." Just reading the titles conjured up diagrams of engine blocks and carburetors and brake drums. He imagined himself talking with a man, older than himself, who was describing a problem with his car.

"The starter turns, but the engine doesn't start. Sometimes the car stalls, and the engine runs roughly. Sometimes it misfires at high speeds, too."

Like a detective, Ryan asks more questions: "Does the engine lack power?"

"Yes," the man would say.

"And does it idle roughly?"

"Yes."

"Hmmm. Sounds like it might be faulty breaker points," Ryan would say. "I'll check it out and give you a call, sir."   The man would flash him a grateful, trusting smile, glad to know someone thought he could find and fix his car's problem.

Ryan's dad was saying something. "... gives some numbers you can call for more information."

"Sorry, Dad, could you repeat that?"

"I just said," his dad replied, trying to mask irritation, "that there's some numbers here you can call for more information about the program."

"This sounds real good, Dad. I think I'd really like to learn about this stuff. I'll call tomorrow morning."

"You might want to look over the catalog tonight," his father suggested. "I'm sure it'll say something about admissions and what you have to do to enroll."

"I'll do that," Ryan said, getting up. "Thanks, Dad. I'm real relieved that you don't mind my not going to a regular four-year

*Don't limit
yourself to
what you've
already done
in your
Positive
Experiences.
Use that
knowledge to
stretch your-
self in new
ways in your
Green.*

college," he added.

"Well, maybe I even owe you an apology," his father said slowly. "I guess I was just too narrow in my thinking. I had a talk with Mr. Hagstrom, and he helped me to understand why you didn't do well in academics, and that that doesn't mean you can't have a good future. It seems plain that your skills lie in a different area than I'm used to thinking about. I want you to do the best you can with what God gave you. And anyway," he said, smiling, "I hear mechanics make better money than lots of college graduates these days. Besides, pretty soon I'll have someone I can really trust to go to when my car rattles and hums. You know how useless I am at fixing things."

"Yeah, but if I fix your car, you know you'll have to do my taxes or something. Just like you always said, you don't get something for nothing in life!"

"Get out of here!" his father said, laughing.

Open Doors, Closed Doors

Ryan and his father both discovered that knowing one's Green and Red areas opens some doors and closes others. Now that Ryan has isolated the skills he both enjoys and does well—building and fixing things—the field of auto mechanics is an open door. He might also find, as he explores his options further, other areas of interest. For instance, electronics. Or heating, air conditioning, and refrigeration. He might want to try his hand at carpentry (building). He knows he likes fixing up cars, because that's what he's already done. But he might try building and/or fixing other things, and see if that provides the same kind of satisfaction.

In other words, don't limit yourself to what you've already done in your Positive Experiences. Use that knowledge to stretch yourself in new ways *in your Green*. By doing so, you will expand your options.

Knowing your Red areas—your "liabilities"—is also tremendously useful. Ryan learned why academics were such a struggle for him—his Red was Ideas, those areas that generally fall into the academic realm. Once he (and his dad) realized there was good training to be had in Ryan's area of strength, he could close the door on the idea of a liberal arts education without feeling guilty. While it's true that almost all fields nowadays require some kind of training after high school, four-year liberal arts programs are just one of the options. Others include the armed services, technical and vocational schools, secretarial training, apprenticeships, and associate degrees in a variety of occupations.

Having said that, we want to stress the importance of getting further training of some kind, in your Green of course. Ryan's dad was right about one thing: Without good training, one's job future looks bleak. You may be sick to death of school right now, but the long-term cost of getting by with only a high-school education is great. Besides, you will probably feel different about pursuing further education if you know it will lead to work you enjoy.

Ryan thought he hated school, but he got excited at the thought of learning more about how car engines work. When you're heading toward your Green, the energy tends to build. And don't underestimate the possibilities your Positive Experiences suggest. Consider Wendy.

People Pay You to Be a Friend?

Wendy was beginning to dread graduation. Most of her classmates were applying to colleges. At her friend Nicole's urging, Wendy had filled out a list of her Positive Experiences. She discussed them in detail while Nicole took notes. Together they worked through the Self-assessment Guide, discovering that Wendy's Green was Relationships, her Red Strategy. But Wendy still felt discouraged.

"All this tells me is that I'm a people person," she told Nicole. "Big deal. I knew that. I still don't know what to do with my life."

"Talk to the guidance counselor," Nicole urged. So Wendy did.

Later that week, list in hand, she entered Mrs. Hartwell's cluttered office and sat down.

"I'm glad to see you," Mrs. Hartwell said with a smile. *She really ought to get her hair cut,* Wendy thought. *I bet she'd look cute in short hair.*

"May I see your Positive Experiences list?"

Wendy handed her the list.

Scanning the paper, Mrs. Hartwell asked Wendy, "As you look at this list, what patterns stand out to you?"

As you may remember, here's what she'd written:

Wendy's Positive Experiences

Period 1: Ages 5-12

Making two "sock babies" from Granny's scrap basket for little brother's birth. (7)

Helping my sister make paper dolls. (10)

Having the best collection of Barbie doll clothes in the neighborhood. (9)

Helping put on a muscular dystrophy carnival with my sisters. (6)

Planning a surprise party for my sister. (3)

Period 2: Ages 13-18

Cutting my sister's hair—and having her like it. (2)

My first job at a beauty salon. (8)

Designing my first dress and wearing it to a school dance. (1)

Befriending a girl in school who was not popular, and helping her become better-liked. (5)

Christmas shopping with my own money, picking out just the right gifts. (4)

Hosting a youth group party. (9)

"I like to work with people," Wendy replied. "But I always knew that much."

"True. But I think this list shows us a lot about *how* you like to work with people. I notice you like to do or make things for other people to make them feel special and cared for (cutting your sister's hair, picking out just the right gift, making sock babies). You also like to create special events that will help other people feel good or special (the youth group party, the surprise party for your sister, planning family vacations). And you like to help other people enjoy themselves, or somehow improve their looks or social standing (the new hair style for your sister, be-friending someone, and helping others to like your new friend too)."

"Yeah, that's me all right—I like to help people have a good time, or to feel good about themselves. But all that means is I know how to be a friend. Who hires anyone to be a friend?"

Mrs. Hartwell said, "Believe it or not, there are jobs that require just the kind of skills you mentioned. A few come to my mind right off: hair stylist; hotel hostess (someone who helps people plan special events); fashion consultant; youth worker. How do any of these possibilities strike you?"

"Well, I enjoy cutting people's hair and just being in the beauty salon where I work," Wendy said. "I've considered becoming a hairdresser. But I don't know if I want to be on my feet all day, working in someone else's shop. I want more freedom. I know that's immature of me, but that's how I feel." Her mother had told her a million times that a person has to be willing to compromise, that someday she'd have to grow up and see that life isn't always a party.

"It's not necessarily immature," Mrs. Hartwell said. "It could be that you need more independence in your work than many people."

Wendy's dark eyes grew thoughtful. "I never thought of it that way. What else did you mention—fashion consulting? That sounds like it might be fun, but I don't really know much about it. I'm always helping my friends pick out clothes and stuff that looks good on them, and I enjoy that. But how do you do that for a living?"

Mrs. Hartwell smiled as she stood up. "You, young lady, have some homework to do. Let's look in the career resource library and see if you can find some answers. You can find out about all the careers I've mentioned, and probably unearth a few more that might be interesting."

Wendy got up. "Sure, I'll go. I still have a few minutes before my next class."

Mrs. Hartwell showed Wendy where the career resource books were in the school library's reference section. She found a few that looked like they might be helpful, most of them in several volumes: *The Encyclopedia of Careers and Vocational Guidance*, and *Career Information Center.* She picked out the first volume of *The Encyclopedia of Careers and Vocational Guidance*, called "Reviewing Career Fields," and looked up "Apparel Industry," "Hospitality," and "Retailing." Each entry gave her an overview of the field, the kinds of jobs available, what the pay and job prospects were, training available, and a list of organizations to contact for further information. Wendy was surprised to see that there was so much good information so easily found.

Even more helpful was the 13-volume set entitled, *Career Information Center.* Wendy picked out Volume 5 to look under "Personal Services." She read, "The area of personal services has three main functions. One is to help people look and feel better. Cosmetologists, massage therapists, and electrologists work toward this goal...." *That's for me!* Wendy thought. She checked the entries under different jobs. *I definitely could become a cosmetologist,* she thought as she scanned the job description. She liked working with hair, liked helping people decide how they would look their best.

Then she came across a job called "Personal Shopper." This must have been what Mrs. Hartwell meant when she said Wendy might become a fashion consultant. Wendy read, "Personal shoppers help busy professional people, usually women, with the time-consuming task of selecting and purchasing clothing and other merchandise. In this emerging field several job titles are used, such as personal shopper, fashion consultant, or personal image consultant." *Wow! Someone might actually pay me to do what I love to do best—shop!* Wendy thought. "Many personal shoppers offer advice on makeup, hair-styling, and colors, in addition to shopping assistance." That's exactly what Wendy wanted to do.

Even better, the book said that such work "does not require any particular education or training, but strong interpersonal skills and a good sense of style are important assets. Experience in retailing and buying is also helpful.... Breaking into the field may involve little more than finding a few initial clients, working with them successfully, and getting permission to use them as references to attract new customers. Working as a salesperson in a clothing store might give you a good start, enabling you either to work your way up to personal shopper for the store or to find your first clients from among the store's customers."

Wendy couldn't wait to tell her friend Nicole the plan that was beginning to form in her mind. She would work in a clothing store, get her own apartment, and start to publicize her services. Maybe she could start with Nicole's mother, who was always complimenting Wendy on her sense of style and bemoaning the fact that she never had time to shop and hated it anyway. Then Mrs. Chandler could tell her friends about Wendy, and, as the book said, her business would be launched. Eventually she'd be able to quit her retail job and work her own hours as her own boss. That would be the life!

The bell rang. Wendy photocopied the pages describing the fields that interested her, stuck them in a file she labeled "My Job Possibilities," and headed toward her next class, head held high.

By now it should be clear to you whether your Green is Strategy, Task, Idea, or Relationship. You should also have a handle on your Green Action Skills. Knowing these things, the next step is to narrow your focus enough to decide on a general career direction, and then discover what kind of further training it requires.

Look at the following list of area/field possibilities in your Green. Circle any that interest you.

Area/Field Possibilities

	STRATEGY	TASK	IDEA	RELATIONSHIP
General Area:	Organizational management, production, promotion	Project administration, support services	Arts, sciences	Human services, support services
Fields:	business consulting competitive sports criminal justice (high-risk situations) finance fund raising investments land development law lobbying manufacturing marketing negotiating politics production promotion purchasing real estate development sales	accounting administrative services assembly work building construction customer service dentistry education/training finance human resources/ personnel industrial engineering nursing (private duty) project administration quality control repair, maintenance safety, compliance systems analysis	architecture art chemistry computer science consulting criminal justice (investigation) design education engineering journalism linguistics mathematics medicine multi-media research science theater/performing arts	administrative services arts/crafts community service counseling criminal justice (when helping is primary) customer service education/training graphic arts hospitality services human resources/ personnel lobbying or purchasing nursing personal services politics psychology public relations public service recreation/sports retail sales travel/hospitality social services

You may notice that some fields show up in several of the S-T-I-R categories. This is because a given field may offer a variety of jobs that call for different skills. Criminal justice is an example. A police officer in the city had better be a Strategy person—someone who enjoys high-risk situations. Other police work may fit the Relationship category, for instance, that of a probation officer. Still another kind of criminal justice work— investigation—would be ideally suited to an Ideas person, someone who likes to gather pieces of data and make sense out of them.

Teaching is another example. A Relationships individual would probably enjoy tutoring, coaching, working with elementary or high-school students. A person whose Green is Ideas would probably need the complexity of college-level teaching to stay challenged. Someone whose Green is Tasks may make a wonderful trainer, doing the kind of teaching that is very practical, very hands-on. So you see, it's important to have a good feel for your Green Action Skills, those verbs that kept showing up in your Positive Experiences. This will help you narrow down your focus in the field that interests you.

In the last chapter, you used your Positive Experiences and some charts to help you identify some of your Green Action Skills. Below is an expanded list of Action Skills possibilities for the S-T-I-R categories. As an added check of your Green Action Skills, circle those that best fit what you did in your Positive Experiences.

If you have a good feel for your Green Action Skills, you can narrow your focus in the field that interests you.

Action Skills Possibilities

STRATEGY	TASK	IDEA	RELATIONSHIP
administer	administer	advise	assist/help
analyze	advise	arrange	befriend/build
build	arrange	befriend	relationships
coach	build	conceptualize	care for/visit
compete	clean	coordinate	coach/develop
control	control	create/invent	conceive
direct	design	design/make	coordinate
envision	edit	investigate	counsel
expedite	facilitate	perform	enable/empower
inspire	keep records	produce	encourage
negotiate	operate	shape	facilitate
organize	organize	study/research	perform
oversee	perfect	synthesize	promote (PR)
perform	problem solve	teach/develop	spark
plan	repair/restore	visualize	supervise/train
promote	serve	write	teach
sell	systematize		
sing	teach		
speak	train/develop		
strategize	troubleshoot		
streamline			
visualize			

Choose Your Field

Both Wendy and Ryan discovered that once they pinpointed their Green—those innate skills they enjoyed using—a little research unearthed career possibilities that excited them.

These lists are not exhaustive. They should, however, help you focus your interests according to your Green Action Skills. If you feel you need more help, you can follow Wendy's example and check out the many resources in your school or public library. Talk with your guidance counselor. Or turn to the list of resources at the back of this book.

Keep Your Options Open

At this point in your life, you want to be headed in the right direction; you don't need a detailed blueprint of your future. If you're not sure what you want yet, it's best to put yourself in the position where your options are as wide open as possible.

Remember Jennifer? When we first met her in Chapter One, she considered becoming a lawyer, a pharmacist, a doctor, a teacher, a journalist, and a musician. After working through her Positive Experiences, she realized Idea was her Green and Task her Red. Based on that information, she ruled out law (Strategy) and pharmacy (mostly a Task job). The other careers would still be open to her if she got a liberal arts education. Once in college, she would have time to explore those other options, finding out more about what the day-to-day duties are in each. She could then compare that information to her Positive Experiences, asking, "Does what this job requires match the kinds of things that showed up in my Positive Experiences?" Step by step, your Positive Experiences can act as a guide throughout your life.

Both Wendy and Ryan discovered that once they pinpointed their Green—those innate skills they enjoyed using—a little research unearthed career possibilities that excited them.

DISCOVER YOUR BEST POSSIBLE FUTURE

Decide on Your Training

OK, you've chosen your direction based on the preceding charts. The next step is to explore your options for further training.

Once Ryan decided on a career—auto mechanics—he needed to find out how best to prepare for that career. He wisely asked other people for their advice. Besides talking to the mechanic at the career fair, he called the mechanic his father went to. He also made an appointment with his school guidance counselor.

For him, the answer was to enroll in a local community college that offered a two-year associates degree in automotive service technology. He discovered that his low grades would not hinder admissions into the community college. With a new sense of direction and excitement that finally he'd be able to do what he enjoyed, Ryan actually looked forward to life after graduation.

Wendy didn't feel so hopeless, either. She planned to take a year off before continuing school; on that she would not budge. But now she had a plan for that year. She would get an apartment and live on her own for a while, to give herself time on her own. She would try to get a job in a high-fashion retail store. She would also start to build a clientele of people she'd shop for, until her client base was large enough so she could quit the store if she wanted. And she would look into some kind of program that would train her in fashion consulting, maybe even cosmetology. Now that she had a goal to work toward, a goal that excited her, she didn't mind going to school for a little more training if she needed it.

College: Yes or No?

For Ryan and for Wendy, a liberal arts college was not the best choice for further training. Their Green abilities suggested other courses of action, courses they could succeed in because they had a plan and were working in their areas of strength.

How do you know if college will be worth the time and expense for you? Check yourself against these qualities:

—Do you have the academic ability to succeed in college?

—Do you have the motivation to apply this ability?

—Do you want to attend college?

—Have you developed good study habits?

—Have you taken the proper high-school program for admittance into college?

If your answer is no to the majority of these questions, you'd do well to investigate alternative forms of training in your Green area. For instance, you could:

—Be accepted into an apprenticeship program.

—Go to a vocational school.

—Take a correspondence course.

—Register for a government training program.

—Enlist in the armed services.

Jennifer and Jeff, however, did plan to go to college. They faced the complex, but not impossible, task of choosing a college. In the next chapter we'll go through the process step by step, taking a look first at how Jennifer chose her school with the help of her dad.

Even if you don't go on to college, you can succeed if you have a plan and work in your areas of strength.

College Choices

JENNIFER FELT HER STOMACH DO FLIP-FLOPS as she opened the envelope containing her SAT scores. She glanced through the hieroglyphics: 1310 total! Not too bad. At this point, since she took the exams in the spring of her junior year, she could always take the test over in the fall and send the better of the two scores to the colleges of her choice. Now she had to figure out what those colleges were.

Knowing that her Green was Idea, and based on her past academic performance, Jennifer wasn't too worried about doing well in school. She liked learning. But she still felt a bit overwhelmed by the many options.

Sitting down in the living room with her parents one night, she confessed her confusion. "There are so many schools out there, and so many college catalogs and stuff. Where do I start?"

Her dad said teasingly, "I can make it real easy on you. We'll look at our bank account and that will rule out about 99 percent of the colleges out there."

Jennifer groaned. "That's another nightmare. Do you know how complicated all that financial aid stuff is?"

DISCOVER YOUR BEST POSSIBLE FUTURE

105

"Yes, we do," her mom said seriously. "You know we've been putting away some money for the last few years. And we really appreciate how responsible you've been about saving. But the cost of college these days is exorbitant; we're going to have to try to find some aid."

"I don't know where to begin!" Jennifer said again.

"Look, let's take this step by step," her dad said. "Didn't you tell me there was a program at school that will give you a list of schools according to certain criteria?"

"Yes, it's a computer print-out you can get from the guidance office. You decide the majors you're interested in and then plug that into a program and the computer gives you a print-out of what colleges offer them."

"Why don't you start there," her dad suggested.

The next day Jennifer went to the Career Resource Center of the library and signed up to use the Guidance Information System computer. When her turn came to use the computer, she discovered there was a dizzying array of variables she could plug in: activities (including sports), characteristics of the college, college size, characteristics of the student body, cost and financial aid, geographic location, majors, special programs, type and size of the community. She hadn't even thought of half of these options!

She decided at this point to just specify some activities (she wanted to make sure there was a Christian group on campus if she attended a secular school), and cost and financial aid. She figured she could always go back and plug in more variables after further research and thought about what she wanted.

Since Jennifer didn't know yet what she wanted to major in, she kept her options open. She wanted a good undergraduate education that would prepare her for the possibility of graduate school later if she decided that's what she wanted. She leaned toward journalism and music, so she typed in those variables also.

The list of schools meeting these criteria was long—dozens of schools! Obviously she would have to narrow her focus.

She showed the print-out to her parents that night. Her mother scanned it, then handed it to her dad. "Looks like you need to get a clearer idea of what you want," she said. "Let's talk about what you'd ideally like, then we can go back and prioritize. Let me get some paper and a pen, and I'll write down what you say."

Her mother returned with pad and pen. She wrote in the top left corner, "School Characteristics."

Jennifer said, "Well, I guess I'd prefer to go to a Christian school, but I'm not stuck on that. I know cost is a factor."

Her mom wrote down, "Christian liberal arts." "What else?" she asked Jennifer.

"I don't really care which part of the country I live in, but I guess I'd prefer to try something different from what I've known. So maybe we should put down 'in or near a big city.' And I want to make sure there are a number of ministry programs in whatever school I choose. And," she added while her mom wrote down what she said, "I want to make sure they have good programs in music and journalism. If I don't major in music, I want to at least minor in it, so it should offer a music minor as well as a major."

Her dad suggested she list everything she wanted in a college, and assign each value a number priority. Five means a college must have it, 0 means undesirable (see chart on page 109). "This way you know just how important each characteristic is," he explained. "It may help later as we compare schools with each other." Then he asked, "Does that computer program you looked at have Christian schools?"

"I'm not sure," Jennifer replied. "I did plug in something about religious affiliation, but I could only choose one, like Baptist. It didn't seem to give me what I needed."

"Is there another resource just for Christian colleges?"

"Yes," she said. "*Campus Life* magazine has a *College Guide* that lists majors and things like that. I saved the last copy. It's in my college file. I'll go get it."

When she returned with the *College Guide,* her dad had another suggestion. "Why don't we make a chart out of this list? We can use the characteristics you listed earlier, and write those down on the left-hand side of the page. Then you can go through the *College Guide* and list the schools across the top that have what interests you. Try to come up with about 10 schools. Fill in your priority numbers alongside each characteristic for all the schools. Sort of our own version of the computer program," he said with a grin.

"That sounds like a good idea," she said. She sat down with the *College Guide,* which contained several helpful articles on what to look for in a college. Then she listed them on the pad.

On page 110 you'll see what her priority list looks like along with her comparison of colleges.

Over the next couple of days, Jennifer consulted the *Campus Life College Guide* and narrowed down her choices to 10 schools. She then wrote to them, asking for more information. As the information came pouring in, she looked over each school's packet carefully. She added the school to her chart, across the top of the paper. If the school seemed to have what she was looking for, she wrote the number in the box for that value.

Jennifer also started a separate file for financial aid information. She was glad she wouldn't have to consider that right away.

By the time Jennifer was through with her chart, she had a number assigned to each school, based on the criteria she had set up for herself beforehand. It's one objective way to measure a school in terms of what you want. That will eventually need to be balanced by visits to your top choices to discover all the intangibles that go into making sure the "fit" of a school is right.

What's Most Important To Jennifer In A College

5 = Imperative, must have   4 = Strongly preferred   3 = Desirable
2 = Acceptable   1 = Undesirable   0 = Unacceptable

	JENNIFER'S CHOICES & PRIORITIES
LOCATION	
Region	
East	0
Northeast	3
Northwest	4
West	4
Midwest	3
South	2
Setting	
Urban	4
Suburban	3
Rural	1
TYPE OF SCHOOL	
Secular	2
Christian	4
Public	2
Private	4
SIZE OF SCHOOL	
Small	4
Medium	3
Large	2
ACADEMIC STRUCTURE	
Entrance Requirements	
Highly competitive	4
Very competitive	3
Competitive	2
Not very competitive	1
Open admissions	0
Majors/minors in my areas of interest	
Strong Journalism	5
Major or Minor in Music	5
STUDENT LIFE (List what is important to you)	
Most students live on campus	5
Off-campus housing available	3
Rules	4
Sports activities	3
Opportunities for ministry	5
Fellowship opportunities	5
....	....
....	....
COST	
Scholarships/grants available	4
Work-study available	3
Loans available	2
How big a factor is cost?	4

5 = Deciding factor   1 = Not a large factor

DISCOVER YOUR BEST POSSIBLE FUTURE

Jennifer's College Comparisons

5 = Imperative, must have   4 = Strongly preferred   3 = Desirable
2 = Acceptable   1 = Undesirable   0 = Unacceptable

Use this chart to compare colleges in terms of the factors you've decided are important.

	JENNIFER'S COLLEGE A	JENNIFER'S COLLEGE B
LOCATION		
Region	*Midwest-3*	*West-4*
Setting	*Sub-3*	*Urban-4*
TYPE OF SCHOOL		
Secular, Christian,	*Christian-4*	*Secular-2*
Public, Private	*Private-4*	*Public-2*
SIZE OF SCHOOL		
Small, Medium, Large	*Small-4*	*Large-2*
ACADEMIC STRUCTURE		
Entrance Requirements	*Compet.-2*	*Hi.Com.-4*
Majors/minors in my areas	*Journalism-5*	*Journalism-5*
	Music-5	*Music-5*
....	....	....
STUDENT LIFE		
Most students live on campus	*5*	*5*
Off-campus housing available	*3*	*3*
Rules	*4*	*4*
Sports activities	*3*	*3*
Opportunities for ministry	*5*	*5*
Fellowship opportunities	*5*	*5*
....	....	....
....	....	....
....	....	....
COST		
Scholarships/grants available	*4*	*4*
Work-study available	*3*	*3*
Loans available	*2*	*2*
How big a factor is cost?	*4*	*4*
5 = Deciding factor		
1 = Not a large factor		
TOTAL	*68*	*66*

How to Choose a College

Using a grid is one effective way to measure a school in terms of what you want.

Let's review some of the steps that Jennifer took in choosing a college.

STEP ONE. *List the schools that provide training in your chosen area.* By now you should have some idea of at least the general field you want to pursue, based on your Green. Jennifer decided to research liberal arts colleges that had strong programs in music and journalism. Jeff wanted a large university with a strong business program and good sports teams (even if he couldn't play, he still wanted to be part of a winning school).

There are a number of resources for finding out what programs schools offer. Many high-school guidance offices can give you a computer printout of schools offering programs in your area of interest. If you're interested primarily in Christian colleges, *Campus Life* magazine publishes College Guide issues in October and March, which list the majors each school offers. There is also a Financial Aid Guide published in December. Other reference books such as *Barron's* and *Peterson's* offer a number of different guides that will help you further refine your list. (See list of resources at the back of this book.)

We suggest you come up with approximately 25 schools that offer what you want academically.

STEP TWO. *Consider your top 10 values—what characteristics you want in a school besides the major.* Do you want to go to a large school (how large?) or small school (how small?) Christian or secular? Private or public institution? In what part of the country? Rural, urban, or suburban?

If you know you may go on to graduate school, you'll want a college that will give you the best opportunity to get into a specific medical or law school or other graduate program. Check into the graduate schools first. Determine what qualifications they desire and what undergraduate institutions they value, and then make your decision.

DISCOVER YOUR BEST POSSIBLE FUTURE

Other factors to consider would be the sports program at a given school; the student/faculty ratio (both within the school in general and the department of your major); whether or not there are opportunities for Christian fellowship and ministry; extracurricular activities; and the living situation. (For example, how many students live on campus? What's the Greek system like? Is there much to do, recreation-wise, on campus, or is having a car a must?)

A big factor, of course, is cost—what can you afford? How much have you already saved? How much can your parents afford to contribute? Are you willing to take out a student loan? What scholarship opportunities exist? (Use the chart on page 115 to prioritize your values).

Some students make the mistake of letting cost be the only determining factor—applying only to the state university, for instance, because it seems the most affordable. We urge you not to do this. Some schools with a higher total cost can actually end up being less expensive because they have more scholarship money to invest in their students. Princeton is one example. It promises that anybody who is granted admission will be able to afford to go. At this early date, you're putting the proverbial cart before the horse if you decide on a school solely because you think you can or cannot afford it.

Consider all these factors, and list those that are most important to you. You might even want to assign a number to each, as Jennifer did, on a scale of one to five, in terms of how important each factor is to you. This may help you later, when you're weighing one school against another. (Use the chart on page 116 for an example.)

STEP THREE. *Gather information about the schools that interest you.* Consult reference books, tapes, slides and other media, viewbooks and brochures, computer programs, college catalogs.

STEP FOUR. *Narrow down your choices according to your top values.* Try to narrow down your choices to eight to ten schools that you can place in your chart. Use your top two or three values to narrow down your choices. For instance, if living in a certain part of the country and going to a private school are your most important factors, find ten schools that fit those criteria. If going to a small Christian liberal arts school is crucial, focus on those schools.

List your ten schools across the top of a chart like the one on page 116 (photocopy chart to add extra schools). Then go down the list and check whether that school has what you're looking for. After you've filled in your chart, you should have a pretty clear idea which are your top three or four that you might want to visit and apply to. (If you're an Ideas person with an interest in math, you might even want to mathematically compute your top schools, adding up all the criteria each school meets according to the priority number you gave each value.)

Use this chart to compare colleges in terms of the factors you've decided are important.

During this narrowing-down step, it's a good idea to visit college fairs and talk to any alumni you may know.

STEP FIVE. *Visit your top schools, if at all possible.* You can find out things in a campus visit that no catalog or brochure can tell you, because you will be interacting with the environment yourself. Try to stay long enough to get a good feel for the campus. Stay in a dorm if you can. Eat in the dorm or cafeteria. Sit in on a class. Talk to the department head of your intended major. Talk to other students. Take notes, because believe it or not, your impressions may begin to blur together once you've visited more than one school!

Note that most campus visits need to be scheduled at least two weeks ahead of time, and that you need to contact the admissions office. It's a good idea to bring someone with you (friend, parents) so you can compare notes.

STEP SIX. *Assemble your paperwork.* It pays to be organized here. (If Task is your Red, enlist the help of a family member or

Try to narrow down your choices to eight to ten schools that you can place in your chart.

friend.) Sketch a résumé of your activities and experiences and a self-portrait of your strengths as a potential college student (handy for application essays and admissions interviews). You already have a great advantage here, because you've already worked with your Positive Experiences.

As the process of college admissions continues, you'll have to send for applications, ask people to fill out recommendation forms, fill out applications, write an application essay, apply for financial aid, perhaps even take more tests. Don't procrastinate! Use the seasonal calendar on page 117 to make sure you're on schedule.

What's Most Important To Me In A College

5 = Imperative, must have   4 = Strongly preferred   3 = Desirable
2 = Acceptable   1 = Undesirable   0 = Unacceptable

LOCATION   MY CHOICES &
Region   PRIORITIES
    East ....
    Northeast ....
    Northwest ....
    West ....
    Midwest ....
    South ....
Setting
    Urban ....
    Suburban ....
    Rural ....

TYPE OF SCHOOL
Secular ....
Christian ....
Public ....
Private ....

SIZE OF SCHOOL
Small ....
Medium ....
Large ....

ACADEMIC STRUCTURE
Entrance Requirements
    Highly competitive ....
    Very competitive ....
    Competitive ....
    Not very competitive ....
    Open admissions ....
Majors/minors in my areas of interest ....
....
....

STUDENT LIFE (List what is important to you)
Most students live on campus ....
Off-campus housing available ....
Rules ....
Sports activities ....
Opportunities for ministry ....
Fellowship opportunities ....
....
....

COST
Scholarships/grants available ....
Work-study available ....
Loans available ....
How big a factor is cost? ....
  5 = Deciding factor   1 = Not a large factor

DISCOVER YOUR BEST POSSIBLE FUTURE

115

My College Comparisons

5 = Imperative, must have   4 = Strongly preferred   3 = Desirable
2 = Acceptable   1 = Undesirable   0 = Unacceptable

Use this chart to compare colleges in terms of the factors you've decided are important.

	MY COLLEGE A	MY COLLEGE B	MY COLLEGE C
LOCATION			
Region	....	....	....
Setting	....	....	....
TYPE OF SCHOOL			
Secular, Christian,	....	....	....
Public, Private	....	....	....
SIZE OF SCHOOL			
Small, Medium, Large	....	....	....
ACADEMIC STRUCTURE			
Entrance Requirements	....	....	....
Majors/minors in my areas	....	....	....
....	....	....	....
....	....	....	....
STUDENT LIFE			
Most students live on campus	....	....	....
Off-campus housing available	....	....	....
Rules	....	....	....
Sports activities	....	....	....
Opportunities for ministry	....	....	....
Fellowship opportunities	....	....	....
....	....	....	....
....	....	....	....
....	....	....	....
COST			
Scholarships/grants available	....	....	....
Work-study available	....	....	....
Loans available	....	....	....
How big a factor is cost?	....	....	....
5 = Deciding factor			
1 = Not a large factor			
TOTAL	....	....	....

Seasonal Calendar

A College Preparation Guide to Help You Know When to Do What

GRADE 10: FALL

Consider taking the P-ACT+, a practice version of the ACT, or the PSAT, a shortened form of the SAT, or "the real thing" (ACT or SAT), just for the experience.

GRADE 10: SPRING

Meet with your high-school guidance counselor.

Choose junior year courses with college entrance requirements in foreign language, math, English, science, etc., in mind.

Investigate advanced placement classes that could earn you college credit.

Consider involvement in extracurricular activities that fit your interests and goals. The experience and skills you pick up will make you more appealing to colleges.

Optional: Take the SAT and/or ACT for practice (if you didn't in the fall).

GRADE 11: FALL

Study hard! This is the last full year of grades that college admissions officers will see.

Register for the PSAT, even if you took it as a sophomore. Juniors with the highest scores in their state may be eligible for National Merit Scholarships.

Consult scholarship directories and college guides, and start visiting college fairs to find out what's available.

GRADE 11: WINTER

Begin browsing through college catalogs to get an idea of where to send your aptitude test scores.

Meet with your guidance counselor, and, with your test scores in hand, discuss what schools you're interested in attending.

Decide when you will take the SAT and/or ACT. If you plan to take either in the spring, register now.

Compile a list of 10 to 15 colleges that appeal to you.

GRADE 11: SPRING

Take the SAT and/or ACT, and any advanced placement tests.

Plan to visit a few different campuses, either during your spring break or shortly after your school lets out.

DISCOVER YOUR BEST POSSIBLE FUTURE

GRADE 12: SUMMER

Request information from various schools.

Sort, file, and organize materials from various schools.

Sketch a résumé of your activities and experiences.

Draft a self-portrait of your strengths as a potential college student.

GRADE 12: FALL

Begin to narrow your list of "choice schools" to no more than eight.

Give any required recommendation forms to selected adults (pastor, teacher, friend) to fill out.

Write the first drafts of your application essay. Have your parents and a couple of teachers proofread it.

Take the SAT and/or ACT (if you haven't already). Or consider taking either test again if you're not satisfied with your earlier scores.

Find out test dates for any other exams required by the schools you're interested in, and register for them.

Send any Early Decision or Early Action applications (often due in November) along with your transcript.

Start work on other applications.

Continue to visit colleges, attending classes and staying in the dorms if possible.

GRADE 12: WINTER

Complete and turn in your high-school transcript and college applications (usually due between January 1 and March 1), especially for financial aid. Note: Your parents must do their taxes before some of the Financial Aid Form questions can be answered.

GRADE 12: SPRING

Once you are notified of your acceptance, decide what school you'll attend and notify all previously-applied-to schools of your choice.

CHAPTER 7

Major Decisions

IF YOU'VE WADED THROUGH THE SEA of college catalogs, calloused your fingers filling out application forms, taking tests, and writing essays, chosen and been accepted by a college—congratulations! The next step is wading through the course descriptions, registering for classes, and settling into a whole new life. In the next chapter we'll go into how you can use your Greens to become a better student. Right now, you're probably wondering about that next big step: choosing a major.

Maybe you already know what major you want. But even if you don't, relax! You've got time. Most colleges require you to take a core of required courses in your first two years anyway, so you'll have time to get used to college life and sample different classes before you must declare a major.

Your Positive Experiences will again be your guide in choosing a major field of study. Knowing your S-T-I-R category has helped you narrow down your choices to a general field of study (Field/Area Possibilities chart). By taking a close look at your Positive Experiences, you should be able to detect some patterns that make it fairly clear what major would lead to satisfying work.

DISCOVER YOUR BEST POSSIBLE FUTURE

119

Let's look at some examples, starting with Jeff.

Jeff Considers a Major

Jeff knew he didn't have to decide on a major before he chose a college. He did, however, want to at least decide between the two areas that seemed to be the most logical choices: business and physical education. That way he could choose a college that had a strong program in his field. (Remember, Jeff is Strategy, and he's motivated by winning. Second best just won't do for Jeff!)

Here, once again, is the list of Jeff's Positive Experiences:

Jeff's Positive Experiences

Period 1: Ages 5-12

Hitting a home run in Little League. (4)

Became popular and leader in our neighborhood even though we had just moved to a new area. (5)

Admitted to the Order of the Arrow, a special group within Boy Scouts. Made more badges than anyone else. (3)

Winning student council election in fourth grade. (8)

In sixth-grade gym class, my team never lost no matter what sport we played. (2)

Period 2: Ages 13-18

Voted "best actor" in sophomore English class. (9)

Getting on the football team and playing varsity. (1)

Selling candy to raise money for our youth group. (10)

Serving as president of a regional high-school church conference. (6)

Working on the school yearbook. (7)

Jeff has already pinpointed his Green Action Skills as competing and winning, overcoming obstacles, and being in charge. His Green is Strategy, his Red is Task.

In order to decide between phys ed and business, he decided

to talk to his high-school phys ed teacher, and some business people from his church.

His conclusions? Phys ed would keep him active and he would be in charge, but the job itself didn't seem to include enough of the direct competing that energized him. Besides, he didn't think he'd like working in a school setting. Business, on the other hand, would offer competition, being in charge and overcoming obstacles—if he got into sales or marketing. One of his Positive Experiences involved selling; several involved managing people and projects. Jeff decided to look for a college with a degree in business, perhaps marketing. Sports he could fit into his life in other ways, he decided. (More about that in chapter nine).

Patterns Pave the Way

To give you a feel for how Positive Experiences can suggest a major, here are some other examples of majors people chose, based on their Positive Experiences. In each case, the PEs are listed chronologically, with the earliest first and the more recent last. Can you see why each person chose what he or she did?

BRYAN
- Playing on a championship Little League team.
- Making money on a paper route.
- Swimming a mile at Boy Scout camp.
- Coaching and playing in a summer softball program.
- Being a counselor at a sports camp.
- Winning a two-mile track championship.
- Playing soccer, half-back ... also helped the coach.
- Getting good grades in twelfth grade.

Green: STRATEGY   Major: PHYSICAL EDUCATION

CARLA

- Taking walks, looking at ants/bugs through a magnifying glass.
- Bird watching with my uncle.
- Taking care of the neighbors' animals.
- Being in the advanced math classes.
- Raising puppies; took care of them if they got sick.
- Science and botany projects ... nature walks.
- Working as an accountant's assistant at a food store.
- Biology and math classes, always got A's.

Green: IDEA Major: BIOLOGY, PRE-MED

DAVID

- Building a tree fort.
- Creating and building my own toys.
- Designing and contracting a special water tank.
- Redesigning a mini-bike.
- Helping overhaul a VW engine.
- Interested in solar collectors; designed one.
- Getting good grades in math and mechanical drawing.

Green: IDEA Major: ENGINEERING

ALLISON

- Directing a play; "coached" younger kids.
- Learning how to make desserts for my family.
- Tutoring a handicapped neighbor.
- Being social chairperson of my youth group with a friend.
- Coaching our freshmen field hockey team.
- Teaching a kindergarten class in our church.
- Speaking to a Rotary group.

Green: RELATIONSHIP Major: EDUCATION

ROB

- Taking care of my blind grandmother.
- Helping Mom take care of my younger sister—she was sick a lot.
- I was "special assistant" to a camp nurse.
- Mowing a big lawn myself.
- Working part-time as a helper in a nursing home.
- Trainer's assistant for the wrestling team.

Green: RELATIONSHIP   Major: NURSING

TIFFANY

- Reading science fiction.
- Building complicated models.
- Making my own clothes.
- Doing well in school, especially arithmetic.
- Fixing my dad's home computer.
- Getting A's in math and chemistry.
- Editor-in-chief of school newspaper, ninth grade.
- Making a 5-foot by 5-foot wall hanging.

Green: IDEA   Major: COMPUTER SCIENCE or MATH

RICK

- Cleaning our house twice a week; both my parents worked.
- Organizing my desk drawers in my bedroom.
- Setting up stereo equipment throughout our house.
- Setting up a mini-catalog order business.
- Keeping neatest shelves as a stock boy at the supermarket.
- Treasurer for our youth group for three years.
- Putting together a "family tree" scrapbook in chronological order.

Green: TASK   Major: ACCOUNTING

*As you look
again at
your
Positive
Experiences,
what majors
come to
mind?*

As you can see from these examples, a number of majors can fit each S-T-I-R category. Knowing whether you are Strategy, Task, Idea, or Relationship is a beginning; the Positive Experiences themselves point to a logical choice in terms of major.

Look for the recurring patterns in your PE's. What were you doing in most of your PE's? What were you working with? What results were you trying to achieve? As you look again at your Positive Experiences, what majors come to mind? Ask yourself these questions, and come up with two or three possibilities. (If the answer is obvious, that's fine; your choice is easy!) Talk to your parents, your academic adviser, and anyone else who knows you well and knows something about what each field entails.

If you've already chosen a major, but suspect it's not the right fit, don't despair—and don't stay with it just because you've already taken some courses in it. Consider Charlene's situation.

Switching Majors

Charlene had chosen counseling and social work as her majors. By the end of the first semester of her junior year at a small liberal arts Christian college, she was ready to quit. She hated her courses. During her Christmas break she told her parents she didn't think she should waste their money anymore.

Her parents listened carefully. Because they were familiar with the approach we've described in this book, they urged her to list her Positive Experiences. "Let's take a look at those and see if they shed any light on why you're unhappy," her mom said. Charlene agreed to take that step before she made any final decision.

Charlene thought long and hard about what to list in her Positive Experiences. The more she thought about it, the clearer the reason for her present unhappiness became.

Charlene's Positive Experiences

Period 1: Ages 5-12

Learning songs, acting out parts, and singing. (7)

Playing in the snow, acting out fairy tales. (8)

Performing in a grade school play. Had one of the leads. (4)

Learning to play the guitar, writing songs and singing them in church. (5)

Period 2: Ages 13-20

Having my own singing group. (2)

Creating a folk mass. (3)

Singing weekends at a restaurant. (6)

Singing solos; I write my own songs. (1)

Take a look at Charlene's Positive Experiences. Can you see why she wouldn't like her psychology and sociology classes?

"Look at this—all my Positive Experiences involve creating and performing!" Charlene exclaimed, bursting into the family room where her parents sat on the sofa together, watching television. "Maybe I shouldn't have given up drama club after all!"

Her parents looked at the paper she handed them. "I'd say maybe you should do more than just get back into drama club, based on these," her dad said.

"What do you mean?"

"I mean, all your Positive Experiences involve singing, acting, or creating. And you have done very little of that in the last year, in school or out," her dad replied.

"You know, now that I think about it, I began to feel unhappy when I dropped my singing and the drama club," Charlene said. "I really wanted to try out for the musical this year, but I just got too busy, I didn't think I could keep up my grades and go to all the rehearsals."

Her mom said, "I remember last year when we talked about

why you wanted to major in social work—you wanted to help people. But helping people doesn't show up on your Positive Experiences list at all. Why did you think you wanted to major in social work?"

"I guess I just didn't think singing and performing were serious enough, or Christian enough," she replied slowly. "I thought I should pick something that would help people more directly."

"I wish we had known about this method a year ago, when you were deciding your major," her mom said. "We would have had a better idea of your talents—talents we think God has given you. I guess we never knew quite how important your performing was to you."

"I didn't either," Charlene said. "It was always just a fun thing to do; I didn't think of making a career of it."

"We believe that if you seek ways to use the talents God gave you, he will provide the opportunities," Charlene's mom said. "You have a wonderful voice, and you can act. Who knows where that may lead? At this point, you need to pray about what this information might mean in terms of your major."

Her dad said, handing her the list, "Maybe you need to talk to your academic adviser about switching majors to something more in keeping with what you have here. Take some drama classes and see if your attitude toward college improves. Give it another semester, and then we'll talk again. The worst that could happen is you'll have to go an extra semester to make up some courses."

Charlene gave each of her parents a quick hug. "Thanks. I feel a lot better about all this." She went into her room, picked up her guitar, and was soon picking out chords to a song that was coming to her. It felt so good to let herself do this again! Why had she let the pressure of school squeeze out the things she most loved to do? She felt hope and excitement building up in her, spilling over in a new song.

If you, like Charlene, find yourself in a major you hate, your

Positive Experiences should pinpoint the problem and clarify a new direction. Don't stay stuck. Better to "lose" some time and money now than years down the road. Many adults are in jobs that are Red for them because they never switched their field of study when they could. Then, degree in hand, they continued in the wrong direction because that's what they had been trained to do. The situation never has to be hopeless—one may find ways to structure some Green into an otherwise Red job. But why not choose the best whenever you can?

Speaking of the best ... has anyone ever told you that your high-school and college years are "the best years of your life"? That's not true for everyone. What helps tremendously, as you weather the ups and downs of these years, is having a settled sense of being in God's will. But how do you find God's will? How can you be sure that the many decisions you must make during these years are wise? In the next chapter we'll address these important questions.

Decision-making and God's Will

NO ONE HAS TO TELL YOU THAT DECISION-MAKING is an important part of life—at this point, you may feel like you're drowning in a sea of important, potentially life-shaping decisions! In this book we've given you a number of tools to make wise decisions about general areas of study to explore, whether or not to attend college, and how to choose the right college and major. Our system is based on the belief that God has created you with certain gifts and tendencies, and discovering what those are is a big part of discovering his best for you vocationally.

Even after you've worked through some of these questions, though, the problem of choosing between two or more attractive options will inevitably arise. Jennifer found that to be the case when she narrowed down her college choices to two equally attractive schools. She felt stymied. She wanted to feel certain of making the right choice in God's eyes. How could she know which school he would want her to attend?

Let's look at some general principles for discerning God's will and making a wise decision. Then we'll see how Jennifer worked through her dilemma, using these principles.

DISCOVER YOUR BEST POSSIBLE FUTURE

129

Finding Out God's Will

First of all, know that God himself eagerly wants to guide you. In Isaiah 42:16 God promises, "I will lead the blind by ways they have not known, along unfamiliar paths I will guide them; I will turn the darkness into light before them and make the rough places smooth. These are the things I will do; I will not forsake them." Again and again in Scripture, we find a variation on this fact: "For this God is our God for ever and ever; he will be our guide even to the end" (Psalm 48:14). (Other verses to explore: Psalms 73:24 and 139:10; Proverbs 4:11; Isaiah 58:11; John 16:13.)

His will is not some mystery hidden in a secret code. He invites us to ask him to reveal himself: "Call to me and I will answer you and tell you great and unsearchable things you do not know" (Jeremiah 33:3). James 1:5 says, "If any of you lacks wisdom, he should ask God, who gives generously to all without finding fault, and it will be given to him." The first step in discovering God's will is to pray for him to give you his wisdom.

You might discover as you pray that, if you're honest, you might not really want his will. What if he wants you to go be a missionary in China, when what you really want is to be an engineer here?

In this case, you may need to start by praying for God to help you be willing to do his will. Two things really help in this: understanding more about the kind of person God is, so that your trust in him increases; and understanding a little bit more about how he's likely to guide you toward career decisions in particular.

To understand more about the nature of God, study his Word. Meditate on the Scriptures already mentioned about how eager he is to be your Guide. Read a book like *Knowing God* by J. I. Packer or *Knowing the Face of God* by Tim Stafford. Study other Scriptures that describe God as a loving Father (Luke 15:11–32); as a tender Shepherd guiding his sheep (Psalm 23; Isaiah 40:11;

John 10:1–18); as a solid Rock upon which we can confidently build our lives (2 Samuel 22; Psalm 18; 1 Corinthians 10:4).

Because God loves you and only wants what's best for you, you can let go of any fear that he may lead you to a bad place. Romans 8:28 declares, "And we know that in all things God works for the good of those who love him, who have been called according to his purpose." And what is his purpose? "To be conformed to the likeness of his Son" (verse 29).

This brings us to an important point: God is more concerned about *who you are* and who you become than the specifics about what, where, and with whom in any decision. Much of what God wants you to do is already revealed: It's in the Bible. In his Book he tells us what kind of people he wants us to be and much of how that is to happen. If the first step is to pray for wisdom, the second step is to know what kind of a person God wants you to be. Then as you face decisions about college and career, try to think through the consequences and implications of each alternative.

For instance, if you're trying to decide on a college, and one of your choices is a school famed for its party atmosphere, you have to ask yourself if this is the best place for you to grow spiritually. You may not rule out that school completely—it may be that you could live off-campus with some Christian roommates, for instance. But it would be foolish to go to that kind of a school without thinking ahead carefully about how you can arm yourself spiritually against the temptations that will inevitably be there. And all other factors being equal, it would be wiser to choose a different college that would not present the same temptations.

Because God loves you and only wants what's best for you, you can let go of any fear that he may lead you to a bad place.

God's Will and Your Green

Besides God's Word, the biggest clue to the kind of work God wants you to do lies in your design, as we've said. You go with the Green, because those are the unique abilities God the Designer has built into you.

The design reveals the designer's will. If I built a car, and asked you, "How are we going to use it?" you might suggest a number of uses for it. We could use it to drive to work, to haul our stuff across country to a new school, or to drive inner-city kids to day camp in the summer. Whatever you suggest, it will involve transportation, because that's what a car is made to do. But you would probably look at more than the fact that it's a car; you would probably look at what type of car it is. Is it a station wagon or van? Then you would know it would be suited to hauling your worldly possessions across country, or inner-city kids to day camp. Is it a Corvette? That would suggest very different uses (you probably would not be able to haul much stuff in it, and certainly not many kids). So: the Design determines the best way something is to be used.

You have already discovered some important things about the way God designed you. As you seek work in your Green areas, pursuing your deepest desires and ways to express the gifts God has given, you can be confident you're following God's will. When God evaluates you as a worker, he will not compare you with other people, but with how faithful you were with what he gave you (see the parable of the talents, Matthew 25:14-30).

There are, however, a few other principles that will help you narrow down your focus. The work you choose must be within God's moral law, as revealed in the Bible. It is not God's will that you become a bank robber, just because "high-risk situations" are Green for you! Any job or career that requires you to violate Christian standards cannot be God's will.

In their book *Your Work Matters to God,* Doug Sherman and

William Hendricks offer another useful guideline. They suggest the work you choose should be of some value to other people. In saying this, we don't mean that it has to be directly involved with people (Relationships is not everyone's Green). But it should somehow serve the needs of people. This value is one that many people don't consider. They look for what the career can contribute to them, in terms of money, status, or security. But a Christian, while considering these things, will be more influenced by what a job can contribute to the needs of other people.

Speaking of other people—other Christians are a great resource for working through the decision-making process. There is a storehouse of wisdom in mature Christians who seek to follow God. Talk to such people; share your concerns and questions; really listen to what they have to say and why they are saying it. Their input is part of the way God intends to guide you. Proverbs 13:10 says, "Wisdom is found in those who take advice." Let's see how Jennifer worked through her dilemma of which school to choose, using some of these principles. Then we'll summarize the steps to making wise decisions.

Which College to Choose?

Jennifer had done her homework as described in the last chapter, and boiled down her choices to two schools. Both had accepted her, both offered good financial aid packages. However, they were very different in every other way, and she was having trouble deciding which she wanted.

School A was a small, Christian liberal arts school near her home town. Though it was more expensive tuition-wise, she figured that would be offset by being able to live at home. The school offered majors in the main fields she was interested in, journalism and music. Important Christian leaders came and spoke at the chapel services. There were also numerous ministry

Other Christians are a great resource for working through the decision-making process.

opportunities open to students. This college had an excellent reputation and she knew she would get a solid Christian education.

School B was a large, secular university with a reputation for having the best journalism program in the country. That of course attracted her—as did the fact that it was on the west coast, in a beautiful setting near both the beach and mountains. She had visited the school and fallen in love with the campus. While there, she had also checked whether there were any Christian groups on campus. There were three very active groups. There were also a number of strong churches near campus. Financially, the school itself was pretty affordable (she had worked out a financial-aid package), though the extra cost of transportation to come home for breaks had to be factored in.

Jennifer felt stuck. She wanted to feel certain of making the right choice in God's eyes. How could she know which school he would want her to attend?

Once again she turned to Tom, her youth pastor, to help her think through the options. As they nibbled on chips and salsa at a Mexican restaurant, Jennifer explained her dilemma to Tom.

"It all seems to come down to which school is better for me, a Christian or a secular school? And I don't know how to choose," she said with a sigh. "Of course I've prayed about it. But I don't feel clear yet on an answer. I keep weighing the pluses and minuses, and the two options seem to be equal. Should I just flip a coin?"

Tom pulled out a quarter. "Heads it's School A, tails it's School B." He flipped the coin, caught it, turned it over and solemnly presented it to Jennifer. "Heads," he said. "Guess that settles that."

"Right," Jennifer said, laughing. "I wish it were that easy."

"OK, OK, I'll get serious," Tom said, pulling his face into a studious expression. "What you really need to decide is what you want."

Jennifer just looked at him. "What do you mean? I want to pick the best school for me, that's what I want."

Tom shook his head. "No, I mean what do you want most from your four years of education? I know the values you listed on your chart. Those are characteristics of a school, and it's important to look at those. But what do you want out of the next four years of your life?"

"Well," Jennifer said slowly as she repeatedly dunked a chip in some salsa, "I want a really good education, of course. One that would lead to a job where I can make a difference."

"Good," Tom said. "What else?"

"I want to be in an environment where my faith can really grow. I want to be challenged. I want to meet different kinds of people and try some new experiences." She noticed Tom was jotting down notes in a small notebook he often carried.

"Anything else?" he asked.

"I think I want to be on my own," she said, then looked surprised. "I didn't even really know I wanted that so much, but I guess I do."

"Anything else?" Tom asked again.

"Well, there are lots of things. I'd like to find a husband. You know, get my MRS degree," she said with a smirk.

"I know you're joking," Tom said, "but actually this is something to consider: The next four years aren't just about getting an education. You're trying to decide what kind of world you should enter. And part of that decision is realizing that in college you'll be forming a network of people that may help you long after you're out of school. And lots of people do end up marrying someone they meet in college."

"Well if I look at it that way, isn't there more of a chance of meeting a lot of Christians at a Christian school?"

"Not necessarily," Tom said. "At least I believe that if you're in the place God wants you to be, then he can make sure you meet the person you're supposed to meet."

Jennifer said, "But that's the whole problem! I'm trying to decide where God wants me, and I don't seem to come up with

The next four years aren't just about getting an education. You're trying to decide what kind of world you should enter.

any answers."

"Oh, we're making progress," Tom said. "See, the first step is to decide what you really want. I have down here: 'Get a good education in my field; be prepared to get a job that would make a difference in the world; grow spiritually; be challenged; meet new people; try new experiences; be on my own; meet Christian men.' "

"You wrote that last thing down?"

"Why not?" Tom said. "Nothing wrong with wanting that to be part of your college experience. If it really doesn't matter to you, I can take it off the list. But if it's important, I think we should leave it on."

"OK, leave it on," she said with a smile. "Now what?"

"Now we eat," Tom said. "And we compare School A with your list of what you want."

Jennifer looked at the list. "Well, School A will give me an excellent Christian education. And there will probably be lots of opportunities to discover ways to make a real difference in the world. I'm sure I will grow spiritually at a Christian college more than at a secular one—"

"Not necessarily," Tom interrupted. "I've been to both seminary and a secular school for my undergrad degree, and I can tell you you can grow in either place or lose it all spiritually at either place. At a Christian school, you can get complacent. You assume everyone's Christian (which isn't necessarily true), and you can get real comfortable and forget that there are lots of hurting people out there. At a secular school, you know you're in the midst of a spiritual battle. You see despairing people all around you who you know need the gospel. Of course, you have to be spiritually strong to withstand the added pressures to fall into the lifestyle you see—lots of partying, drinking, sex. But if you're part of a good Christian fellowship group, it can help a lot.

"All that to say you shouldn't assume that you will automatically grow more, spiritually, at a Christian college."

"I guess I hadn't really thought it through," Jennifer admitted. "But isn't it true that, what with all the great speakers and Christian teachers, there is the opportunity to really be stretched in my faith?"

"No doubt about it," Tom said. "It's really up to you and what you want to make out of it."

"OK, let's look at the rest of the criteria. I would meet new people at School A, but they probably wouldn't be from a wide range of different backgrounds. I think there are opportunities to try new experiences. And certainly I would get to meet Christian guys. The big drawback is I would have to live at home, and I would probably not feel like I'm on my own as much as if I lived in a dorm."

Tom asked, "Is living in a dorm out of the question?"

"It seems like it. I'd be stretched to the max as it is, just to afford tuition at School A, even with a scholarship."

"OK, let's move to School B," Tom suggested.

"Well, it looks like that school too would have everything I want. But I'd be completely on my own—maybe too much so! It would be so different and so far away ... I wonder if I'm ready."

"Only you can decide that," Tom said. "For what it's worth, you seem pretty mature to me, and you seem to be able to handle new situations well."

"Thanks, Tom. I know I could do it. It's just ... so many of my friends are going to School A, or some other Christian college, it's tempting just to go along."

"Usually the best decisions are made when there are more than two options. Is there a third you can think of?"

"The major drawback with School A is I wouldn't be on my own enough. Maybe I could live in a dorm the first year, just so I really feel I'm part of the school scene and so I can meet people. Then maybe it wouldn't be bad to live at home for the rest of the time."

"That's a good option to explore. Or maybe you would be able to afford an apartment on campus. Lots of times a family

*We can
weigh all
the pros
and cons of
a decision,
but in the
end it comes
down to a
subjective
decision.*

will give you a room for very little rent, or you can even do something like housework or baby-sitting to offset some of the room and board expenses. So you've got two variations on School A that take care of the problem with School A and will still allow you to reap all the advantages of going there.

"Now let's compare all these options with each other," Tom said.

As they continued to talk things through, Jennifer found herself getting excited about the thought of going away to a whole new area of the country. It would be scary, certainly. She knew she would be homesick. But something inside her wanted to take the plunge.

"You know, we can weigh all the pros and cons of a decision," Tom responded, "but in the end it comes down to a subjective decision. I'm sure you will do well with either of these choices. You've prayed about it; you've thought through the consequences as best you see them at this point; now it's time to make a choice and trust God will be with you in that."

Decision-making at a Glance

Let's review the steps Jennifer took in deciding which college to go to. These steps will help you in any decision you need to make.

1. Pray. You can pray for God's wisdom in showing you the specifics of your design and what opportunities will best fit that design. You can pray that God will show you if a situation or opportunity might tempt you to compromise your standards. You can pray about which opportunities will contribute to the needs of others.

As you pray, be open to God speaking to you through his Word, through the insights of others, and through your own inner convictions.

2. Seek God's counsel (though his Word) and the counsel of mature Christians. As Jennifer studied God's Word, she became convinced that a priority for her must be to make sure the school she chose would enable her to grow spiritually. She would not have considered the secular college at all if it didn't have strong Christian groups on campus and churches that would provide her with fellowship and Christian teaching. And as she talked with Tom and others, she gleaned valuable feedback on their perception of her maturity. Talking out the options also helped Jennifer clarify what she really did and didn't want.

3. Clarify what you want most—your objective. This may seem obvious, but too often people just jump right into comparing options with each other, without ever really clarifying what they want. For career decisions, make sure your objective incorporates the three criteria mentioned: Is it in your Green? Is it within God's moral laws? Does it allow you to contribute in some way to the needs of people?

4. Study the situation or problem. Jennifer had done her homework on what each school had to offer, and she thought through the consequences of what going to each would mean for her.

5. Compare Alternative A with the objective. Sometimes when you do this, you'll realize that Alternative A really doesn't meet your objectives at all. You save yourself a heap of time when you first compare your alternatives with your objective.

6. Compare Alternative B with the objective.

7. Discover Alternative C. You make the best decisions when you have at least three alternatives, so make sure you think of at least three attractive options. In coming up with other alternatives for School A—options that would take care of the problem of not being on her own—Jennifer realized she really didn't want to go to School A as much as School B.

8. Compare Alternative C with the objective.

9. Now compare all three (or more) alternatives with each other. Here is where you evaluate the pros and cons of

For career decisions, make sure your objective incorporates the three criteria mentioned: Is it in your Green? Is it within God's moral laws? Does it allow you to contribute in some way to the needs of people?

each choice with the others.

10. Pick the most attractive alternative.

11. Take action, trusting that God will be with you.

Decision-making and Your Style

Depending on what your Green is, you'll have a tendency to get bogged down in one or more of the above steps. Knowing your potential area of weakness can help you stick to the parts of the process that are less natural to you.

For instance, Strategy people may not take the time to clarify their objective, and instead may concentrate on comparing all the alternatives. Because their decision-making tends to be quick, they may not take the time to think through the problem or situation.

Task people may get too caught up in comparing the alternatives. Idea people may get snagged by overanalyzing the problem. Relationship people may be too dependent on the advice and feedback of others, and also may not take the time to clarify objectives and think through the problem. These are just generalizations; a little bit of thought about past decisions you've made will probably point out where your weaknesses lie.

If you can learn how to pinpoint your Reds and work around them, you're way ahead of many other people. In the next chapter, we'll look at how to get the most out of your school years by working with both your Reds and your Greens in the job you currently hold—the job of student.

Making the Most of Your Education

KNOWING BOTH YOUR GREEN AND RED areas gives you a definite edge in getting the most out of your education. And not just academically, but socially and personally as well. It will help you learn how to set realistic expectations (and thus guard your self-esteem), build on your strengths, and discover how to approach your responsibilities with the style that works for you. All these skills will help you build a satisfying life, well beyond your school years.

Current Job: Student

Think of being a student as a job. Many different responsibilities make up this job: studying, taking tests, writing papers, establishing good study habits, attending classes, making friends, doing independent projects, working with others to complete a project, taking SATs and other standardized tests, living with a roommate. Some of these tasks will be Green for you, some will be Yellow, some Red, depending on whether you're Strategy, Task, Idea, or Relationship. For instance, in general, studying is Green for Idea,

DISCOVER YOUR BEST POSSIBLE FUTURE

Yellow for Strategy, Yellow to Red for Task, and Red for Relationship people.

Below is a chart that breaks these responsibilities down and matches each S-T-I-R category with how difficult or easy that task will tend to be. There will always be exceptions—not all Idea people enjoy studying, for example, especially if the subject doesn't interest them. But this chart may help you understand and anticipate areas of struggle as well as your strengths in your career as student.

Student Job Responsibilities

Responsibilities	STRATEGY	TASK	IDEA	RELATIONSHIP
Studying	RED	YELLOW	GREEN	RED
Taking tests	GREEN	RED	YELLOW	RED
Writing papers	RED	RED/YELLOW	GREEN	RED
Working under pressure	GREEN	RED	YELLOW/RED	RED
Developing good study habits	RED	GREEN	GREEN	RED
Attending classes	RED	YELLOW/GREEN	GREEN	RED
Socializing	RED	RED	YELLOW	GREEN
Competing (curve raising)	GREEN	YELLOW	YELLOW	RED
Independent learning	YELLOW	GREEN	YELLOW/GREEN	RED
Taking standardized tests (SAT, ACT)	GREEN	RED	YELLOW/GREEN	RED
Living with roommate(s)	YELLOW	RED	YELLOW	GREEN
Overall matchup	YELLOW	YELLOW/RED	GREEN	RED

As we can see, the overall job of being a student tends to be Green for Idea people, Yellow for Strategy, Yellow to Red for Task, and Red for Relationship people.

Living with Your Red

Being a student will be most difficult for Relationship people, but no matter what your S-T-I-R category, some aspect of being a student will be difficult for you. In fact, we all have to deal with our Red areas on a daily basis, because there will always be responsibilities we don't enjoy that we have to do anyway. All along we've been encouraging you to "go for the Green." But how do you deal with the Reds in your life?

Remember, a Red is the opposite of a Green: Red means we will have to work harder, the task will take longer, and we will never do it at as high a level as we would if it were Green or even Yellow. The key to living with your Red is knowing what is Red for you, and holding realistic expectations of yourself when faced with a Red.

You shouldn't expect yourself to perform at A level in your Red. You should expect the task to take at least twice as long as you think it will take. You should expect to put more effort into your Red, and not feel bad when despite a lot of effort you perform at B or C level. In fact, you could feel very proud of B-level work in your Red.

If you know your Reds and adjust your expectations accordingly, you can save yourself a lot of grief. If at the same time you make sure you have some Green in your life, you'll be able to get through your school years, no matter how much of your job is Red for you.

Let's look at how Jeff made some decisions about his first year of college, based on what he knows about his Green and Red areas.

Red means we will have to work harder, the task will take longer, and we will never do it at as high a level as we would if it were Green or even Yellow. The key to living with your Red is knowing what is Red for you, and holding realistic expectations of yourself when faced with a Red.

DISCOVER
YOUR BEST
POSSIBLE
FUTURE

143

Decisions in a Red and Green Light

By this time, Jeff has entered a large university in the Northeast that has both a strong football and soccer team, and a decent basketball team. Though he can't play, of course, because of his injured knee, he plans on seeing as many games as possible. Sports, which fall in the field of Strategy, are Green for him. It makes sense that they would dominate his social and recreational life. He is even thinking of looking into announcing games on the college radio station.

At this point, Jeff isn't sure what he wants to do after college, but he's leaning toward the business world. Ideally, he would like to get into some kind of corporate training program after college. But sales is also a possible entry-level position that he would probably enjoy and do well in. He hasn't ruled out the possibility of majoring in physical education, either. He plans to talk to people in both fields to find out what would be a better match. (More about how Jeff went about making this decision in Chapter 10.)

Idea is Jeff's Red. Does this mean he won't be able to hack college? Not necessarily. What it does mean is that at least certain subjects will not come easily to him. Remember, Red is what you don't like doing and don't do particularly well even if you expend a great deal of effort. If Jeff keeps this in mind, he will expect to have to study harder and longer, at least in certain subjects. And he will have to adjust his expectations for himself. He hopes that once he can concentrate on subjects in his major, he will do A-and B-level work. In the meantime, he's setting his sights on doing as well as possible in his first two years, when he has to fulfill general academic requirements. For him, a C in English and history may be his best work; he can feel satisfied with that. Because he knows his Red, he sets expectations that are realistic for himself. He tries not to compare himself to others who obviously have a natural bent toward academic learning.

Task is also Red for Jeff. Therefore another uphill battle for him is organizing his paperwork and dorm room. As luck (or Murphy's Law) would have it, Jeff rooms with a guy whose Green must be Task; Rob is a neatnick, to put it mildly. All his books and notebooks are organized, not strewn about like they are on Jeff's side of the room. Rob has a big calendar on the wall above his desk, which he uses to keep track of his tests and deadlines for papers. He even writes down how many pages he has to read to keep up with the syllabus.

Rob can't understand why Jeff doesn't adopt his approach to studying. It's obviously the most logical, and it keeps him on track. If Jeff didn't know something about himself and the Green Light concept, he may have felt there was something wrong with him. Now he knows that he works best under pressure. He told Rob so one day, when he explained what he's learned about the Green Light concept.

Rob wasn't too impressed. "I don't see how you can expect to do well on tests if you don't keep up all along," he said. After midterm exams, when Jeff crammed for four days straight, he was inclined to agree. He did rise to the occasion and made a couple of B's and the rest C's, but he had to admit Rob was right. "I seem to be in a catch-22," he told Rob. "I really do work best under pressure, but cramming everything at the end is apparently too much pressure."

"Maybe you can create a little pressure for yourself along the way," Rob suggested. "I'll be the heavy. Set your goals weekly, and write them on your calendar." Jeff groaned. "No, I'm serious. If you write down your assignments, I can check it and get on your case about it. Voilà—instant pressure! Then maybe you'll work at your best and keep a *sane* pace." Jeff looked doubtful, but agreed to try it. And with some periodic prodding from Rob along the way, he found the strategy enabled him to keep up a little better.

Something else helped Jeff. Because he knew he was competitive, he found another guy who was in most of his classes to

Because Idea is a Red for Jeff, he should expect to study harder and longer.

DISCOVER YOUR BEST POSSIBLE FUTURE

145

compete with. He didn't tell Michael he was competing with him; he just talked about his classes with him, casually found out Michael's grades, and secretly tried to better him. Since the two students were fairly evenly matched, it challenged Jeff to do his best work.

As Jeff discovered, there are ways to make your Green work for you even in your Red areas. Let's look at some other tactics to make the core tasks of your job as student easier, even if they're your Red.

If Studying Is a Red for You...

Studying is most difficult for a Relationship person. Does this mean if you're a Relationship person you should forget school altogether and go out and party?

No. What it does mean is that you should make sure your major is in your field—something people-related. Again, it means you understand that you may have to study harder and longer than some other individuals. You can set your sights for an A, study hard, and feel very satisfied with a B. And in the first couple of years of college, when most of your classes will not be in your major, you will have to set your expectations realistically and hold on to the hope that school will get easier. You may have to be extra disciplined not to let socializing crowd out study time.

You can also try to tailor your study approach to your Green. For instance, most Relationship people study better with other people, either in groups or with at least one other person. Study the material yourself first, then talk it over with another person whenever possible.

In the classroom, Relationship people will tend to get bored quickly in lecture-only situations, but they come to life during discussions, especially when interacting with other students. Again, if you are Relationship and you have a choice, pick classes with a discussion format.

Working with Your Reds

If you are a Task, Idea, or Strategy, the academic part of school will be a mixed bag.

Task students will automatically settle into a schedule and routine of specified study times. They are the ones who will write down all their deadlines on a master calendar, and will approach studying systematically, as Jeff's roommate, Rob, did. They live by their schedule and "to do" lists.

The Red areas of being a student for Task people lie in taking tests and building social relationships. If your Green is Task, you already know you don't do well under pressure. Anything you can do to minimize the pressure will help. Obviously, you should not cram for tests. But while taking a test, it may help if you approach it systematically. For instance, look over the test first to get a general "feel" for the test as a whole. Go through and answer all the easiest questions first. By then, you may have become sufficiently engrossed to concentrate on taking the test rather than being aware of the pressure. You may also want to prepare yourself mentally ahead of time by trying to gain perspective on the upcoming test. Ask yourself: "Ten years from now, will I even remember the grade I got on this test?" (This is a question to ask yourself *after* you study, not before! You want to defuse the pressure, not demotivate yourself from studying.)

Task may also find the social part of being a student more difficult. Again, if you can find a way to develop a systematic approach, you've moved your Red toward your Green. For instance, you may decide that you want to overcome your shyness. Set a goal for yourself, perhaps to talk to one new person a day, just briefly. Write down your goals; check them off as you meet them. Seeing yourself make progress may help you to persevere toward your goal.

Idea people may set up a study schedule, but then find themselves falling behind. Why? Because they often lose themselves

*Cramming is
not a good
idea if your
Green is
Task, Idea, or
Relationship.
You'll only
get yourself
in bot water
because
you'll be in
red waters
not green
waters.*

in a subject or get sidetracked by something that interests them along the way. Their learning tentacles are always out, grasping knowledge. They often love lectures and time afterward to question the instructor.

If Idea is your Green, you'll have a comparatively easy time in school. You might as well enjoy it! You will not do well under pressure, so allow yourself plenty of time to study and keep up (as well as time to follow your own interests, if you often find yourself getting sidetracked). The major challenge for you may be to make sure you don't study *too* much. You'll have to work to balance your life with enough socializing and, perhaps, physical activity. Remind yourself that people, too, are a wonderful source of ideas and learning opportunities, and that physical exercise keeps your mind sharp.

Strategy people may set up a study schedule, like Tasks, but then they have to be very, very disciplined to stick to it. They may stay most on target in subjects that interest them. Many will do just enough to get by, then cram at test time. Because of the pressure of the moment, many Strategy people blossom at test time because they are in their Green. But beware! No one can pack a semester's worth of study into one or two nights. If you're Strategy, learn your limits—find out when you cross the line from pressure that energizes you to pressure that paralyzes you. You might try some of the tactics Jeff adopted—finding someone to compete with, at least in your own mind; and creating artificial deadlines along the way so that you feel the pressure is on more often.

Just to repeat—cramming is not a good idea if your Green is Task, Idea, or Relationship. You'll only get yourself in hot water because you'll be in red waters not green waters.

Special Opportunities

No matter what kind of education you're pursuing, there will be special opportunities along the way to broaden your knowledge and gain experience in a field that interests you. Such things as summer opportunities, internships, and semester abroad programs can help you explore an area you think may be in your Green, help you get a head start in college, investigate a career, visit a new place, make friends, and have loads of fun, all at the same time.

When John finished his junior year of high school, he didn't want to face another summer of boredom. He investigated some options, and ended up in a Hollywood movie studio, studying mass media with film professionals. Tracey, another high-school student looking for a change, spent her summer living in a dormitory in Canada, polishing her volleyball skills at the University of Victoria. For both John and Tracey, these experiences taught them a lot about who they were and what kinds of skills they enjoyed using.

There are hundreds of programs at colleges and universities throughout the United States and Canada. Most are open to high-school students who have completed their sophomore or junior year, but many programs are also available to younger students or to graduating seniors.

There is something available for every kind of interest. You can select a program that focuses on just about any academic area, from journalism to mathematics to zoology. Or if you don't want to spend your summer studying, you can pick a non-credit session that is just for fun.

Internships are another important opportunity. Through an internship, you can verify whether you really will like doing a certain job, gain valuable experience, and even, in some cases, earn college credit.

Do whatever you can to use some of these opportunities to test what you know about yourself and explore ways to hone your skills. Just because an area is Green for you, it doesn't mean you don't need further training. At the same time, since you know your Green, it's unlikely you'll choose something that will waste your time or money.

To find out what opportunities are available, check out directories such as *Peterson's Summer Opportunities for Kids and Teenagers* or *Summer on Campus: College Experiences for High School Students.* Also, your school guidance office, the public library, and your school's careers department should have other information about various opportunities.

Off the Job:
Extracurricular Activities

The academic part of your job as student—studying, taking tests, writing papers—may be primary, but it's not all there is to your education. Extracurricular activities, service opportunities, even summer jobs can develop valuable skills that are at least as important to your future as the academic subjects you study and your grade-point average.

Diane's first career job after college was writing and producing a radio show for InterVarsity Christian Fellowship. Her four years of involvement in IVCF as a college student had just as much to do with her getting that job as her major and academic record. Again and again, she found herself calling on the personal, spiritual and relational skills and disciplines she developed through InterVarsity. Don't overlook what extracurricular activities can do for you.

Sometimes the only way to build on your Greens may be through nonacademic activities. Remember Ryan? Schoolwork was not his forte, but building and repairing things gave him great satisfaction. His eventual career direction as a mechanic was based on the interest he kept alive largely outside of school.

How do you know which extracurricular activities to choose? Most high schools and colleges offer a bewildering array. Again, let your interests and your Green guide you. Build on past Positive

Experiences, but don't be afraid to try something new. If you are a Strategy, sports, debate, and business clubs are a natural—anything that encourages competition and pushing yourself to the limit, or speaking before an audience. Task people may enjoy activities that involve skills such as instructing, organizing, or constructing. Idea students may gravitate toward music, drama club, working on the yearbook, photography, tutoring, or teaching. Service organizations are a natural for Relationship people.

Consider Making a Difference

Service opportunities actually offer something for everyone. All service groups can use people in each S-T-I-R category: Strategy people tend to become program promoters, Task people handle projects from A to Z, Idea people offer vision and creative skills, and Relationship people provide fun and help everyone feel they belong.

Consider joining some service organization, whether it's a school club, a church or Christian organization, or a community group. You'll grow as a person, make friends and build your relational skills, and learn a lot. Doing something for others also helps you feel good about yourself—people come to need you, to depend on your input. It's also an opportunity to express your values. Just make sure that when you get involved, your major input is in your Green, whether that means leading, organizing, teaching, or counseling.

Here are some true-life examples of students who wanted to make a difference somehow and found creative ways to do it based on their Green—what they loved to do. What these people accomplished can't help but also pave the way for their own future success and fulfillment.

Making a Difference, Building a Future

• Challenged at a youth convention to make an impact for Christ in her school and community, Sherri Howard rallied fellow high-school students together to start a club they called The Choice. They met for regular Bible study and prayer before school. They sponsored alcohol-free parties as an alternative to the keg parties that were common in their communities. When Sherri later became Kansas's Junior Miss, she began to put on assemblies in elementary schools to help kids say no to alcohol and other drugs.

Sherri is probably a Strategy person. She combined her innate relational skills with her values to make an impact on her school. That impact continued even after she went on to college.

• After a short-term missions trip to Haiti, Rich Wagner wanted to do something concrete to help the people in Haiti. Together with his family, he brainstormed things he liked to do. When biking showed up high on the list, Rich's dad commented, "You could always ride your bike across the country." He was really joking, but Rich began to wonder if maybe he could raise funds that way. His dad helped him prepare a formal proposal for the board of International Child Care (ICC) to authorize his special fund-raising project. The organization agreed to let him raise the money on their behalf with all donations earmarked for a special project to immunize Haitian children with a vaccine against numerous contagious diseases, whooping cough, measles, polio, and others.

Rich raised $10 in pledges for every mile of his 3,000-mile trip from Oceanside, California, to the Atlantic coast outside Boston. A U.S. government agency promised to match what he raised, triple-fold. By the end of his 29-day ride, more than $35,000 came in. With the matching funds added, Rich's ride provided immunization for more than 100,000 children. Not a bad thing to have on your résumé before you're even out of college!

• Todd Peterson began volunteering with Habitat for Humanity on Saturdays because he enjoyed carpentry work and wanted a change from the grind of college life. Habitat for Humanity uses volunteers nationwide to help build homes for people caught in poverty. North Park College's program, the one Todd was involved in, soon grew into a complex organization—and Todd took on more and more responsibility. His most challenging task was to coordinate the material, the work, and the volunteers for the current projects. Though these responsibilities took up 15 to 20 hours of his already-full weeks as a full-time student, he enjoyed it. That's because Todd was working in his Green, on something he believed in.

• As a freshman, Becky Kealy volunteered to be on a committee of students to plan meetings and activities for LIVE, an independent Christian club run by and for students at the San Bernardino, California, high school. At a committee meeting, someone suggested they needed some sort of publicity to help build interest and awareness of the club. Becky had always enjoyed writing, so she volunteered to do a newsletter. The next week she ran off 150 copies of a one-page newsletter announcing the club meeting and highlighting some important upcoming events, with a few riddles and puzzles thrown in for fun. Each week, the LIVE club and the newsletter grew. Becky began including short interviews with Christian students who would give a Christian testimony for the newsletter, or an essay on a spiritual topic. And always there were more riddles, puzzles, and jokes.

Soon teachers and students began asking for copies of the newsletter each week. The club grew, and people from other schools even began asking for copies of the newsletter. Within a year, when Becky was just a sophomore, the one-page weekly newsletter had become a 16-page monthly with a circulation of 4,000 copies distributed to more than a dozen high schools.

Identify Your Passions

Sherri, Rich, Todd, and Becky all started with a strong desire to do something significant for other people, and all found creative ways to turn that passion into reality.

During the years you're completing your education, make sure you get in touch with what you want most in life. Take the time to dream a little, to get in touch with your deepest desires and values. If you could do what you really wanted, what would you do? Not just in your career, but with your life? What kinds of needs, problems, issues concern you that you would like to do something about? What is often on your heart as a deep-seated concern?

As you think about these things, keep your mind wide open. Look at all areas of your life, not just academics. Forget about what you've already done, or what seems possible. Just focus on your deepest desires and convictions. What's important to you in general? What principles won't you compromise no matter what? Don't let what other people have said influence you. Right now this is *your* dream.

If you need some help to jog your mind a bit, try the following exercise.

Exercise:
Pin Down the Dream

Jot down answers to the following questions. Don't spend a lot of time on any answer; just write what first comes to mind.

I would like to be the kind of person who ...

If I could do anything I wanted, without worrying about time or money, I would ...

If I could change one thing in the world, it would be ...

If I knew a drunk driver would smash into my car and kill me five years from today, I would want to make sure I've ...

You might want to summarize your thoughts below.
My interests and concerns, dreams and aspirations:

Most likely, what you wrote above is in line with what you've already discovered about yourself thus far. But maybe you've uncovered new things you'd like to try. Go for it! As we'll see in the next chapter, there are things you need to learn that you'll learn only one way—by doing.

CHAPTER 10

What They Don't Teach You in School

SCHOOL WILL HELP YOU DO LOTS OF THINGS. It can, of course, train you in specific areas you will need to know for a specific field. If you're planning to become a physicist, you have to know about physics, obviously. And school can do some less tangible things for you: It can help you learn how to think for yourself, how to question, how to find out things for yourself.

Indirectly, your years in school can provide the opportunity to develop social skills. Working on projects with others, or on a sports team, will help you learn teamwork. Interacting with teachers and professors helps you learn how to work under authority. All these will be essential to later success in a career.

But there are a few things you may have to unlearn in order to succeed in the world of work. Actually, the sooner you unlearn them, even while in school, the better. Let us explain.

Life Is Not Like School

In school, "good students" are those who do their work "correctly" and are rewarded with good grades and recognition. In ele-

DISCOVER YOUR BEST POSSIBLE FUTURE

mentary school, the emphasis was on learning and parroting back to the teacher the right answer. By the time you hit high school, however, you began to see that not everything has a "right answer"; many areas of life are open to a variety of perspectives and interpretations. Oh, there are still a lot of facts to learn, but more and more you'll be asked to go beyond the facts and interpret what they mean.

Once you're in college, you will be evaluated (graded) on essays, papers, and participation in class discussion more than on simple multiple-choice tests. You'll be expected to think for yourself, to take initiative, to be an active rather than a passive learner.

By the time you're ready to start your career, the fact that you do well on standardized tests will mean nothing. Your degree or certificate will prove that you have mastered a certain body of information. That's only the starting point. If you expect that you'll be hired simply because you graduated magna cum laud, and that you'll move on up the career ladder automatically simply by doing a good job, you'll be disappointed. Those who study successful people have discovered that there are other skills that separate those who succeed and grow in their careers from those who simply do their job and go nowhere.

These two skills are *risk-taking* and *being able to connect with people*. Let's look at some of these skills and see how you can begin to hone them even now, while you are still a student— using your Greens and Reds to your advantage.

Skill #1: Something Risked, Something Gained

By the time you're on your own, you'll quickly realize that no one will hold your hand. Getting a job, then learning how to do it well and solve the problems that come up, will require your own initiative. The sooner you can develop a willingness to try new things, and to chalk up any failures to the proverbial "learning experience," the better off you'll be.

Unless your Green is Strategy, you may not embrace the idea of taking risks. Yet you can hardly get to this point in life without having taken a great many risks. Every time you've tried something new, you have risked failure. But as you have discovered, many times those risks were worth it because they opened the door to opportunities. Even your failures, however painful, taught you something. We hope it's not the lesson "never risk again"! Not only is that an impossible goal—life is full of risks—but it's also undesirable. The only way you can grow is to take risks.

You've seen how it works in sports, in relationships—nothing risked is nothing gained. Those who succeed and grow in their careers, as opposed to those who do their job and go nowhere, are people who are willing to try new things.

We encourage you to take risks in three areas, whenever appropriate: in your Green, in your Red, and in the unknown.

Risk in Your Green

It's always easiest to take risks in your Green, because you have some confidence you'll succeed. Taking risks in your Green can give you valuable practice for taking bigger risks in other areas.

Jeff decided that since he couldn't play sports but still wanted to be involved, he would see if the campus radio station needed a sports announcer. He hadn't heard there was a job opening; it was just something that interested him that he thought he would explore. He figured announcing would be Green for him because it involved speaking and performing, in a way.

The station didn't need anyone right away to cover the sports scene, but they asked if he'd be willing to do some other announcing. He said yes, just to gain some experience, but made

Those who succeed and grow in their careers, as opposed to those who do their job and go nowhere, are people who are willing to try new things.

it clear that his real interest was sports announcing. For a couple of months he played music on the station. But he hung around when the games were being announced to see how it was done. He also got to know the student who did most of the sports shows. When that student decided he needed more time to study, he asked Jeff to take over. Jeff was glad to and found he enjoyed it immensely.

Notice that Jeff went after what he wanted. He wasn't obnoxious. In fact, he settled for something less than what he initially wanted. He used the opportunity to get to know the other radio personnel, to learn about the job, and to be available. Many a job is created or had by just such a strategy.

Charlene also took a risk in her Green. Before she decided for sure to change majors from psychology to drama or music, she decided to try out for a school play. She did get a part. She planned to use the experience to confirm whether she should in fact change majors.

Reaching out for opportunities in your·Green is natural and can help you to build on your strengths. But taking risks in your Red is just as important in a different way.

Hidden Strength in Weakness

Chances are you avoid doing anything in your Red as much as possible. That's natural. It's also impossible to totally avoid your Red. As you already know, every day you have to do things that are Red for you. But consider this: What's Red for you is also the very thing that holds the most potential for personal and even spiritual growth.

God has the most opportunity to display his kindness and power to you in your areas of weakness. Chances are you need to grow a lot in your Red. Setting growth goals in your Red and asking God to help you can increase your faith and help you to change.

For instance: Let's say your Red is Relationship, and you're very shy. Should you say, "Relationships are Red for me, therefore I don't have to talk to people"? If you did, you'd be pretty lonely. No, a better way to handle this is to say, "Relationships are Red for me, but I don't want to be a hermit. I'm going to ask God to help me take the risk of speaking to one person a day. And I'm going to trust him to help me do that." So you pray, asking God for the courage to speak to one person a day. And if you don't reach your goal, that's OK. You're not a bad person or a failure. You remind yourself why it's difficult for you, and you try again the next day. Chances are before long you'll feel much more comfortable initiating conversations. You may never *enjoy* talking to strangers. That's allowed. But you haven't let your Red hold you back from what you really want for yourself—good relationships.

Take another example. Suppose this time your Red is being organized. Does this mean that you give up and drive your mother and your roommate nuts with your messiness? No. It means you set some goals for yourself—modest goals, like putting away all your clothes every night or finding a place for your books. You ask God to help you in this area. Maybe you even ask for help from a friend who is more organized.

Here the "risk" is different. It involves acknowledging you're not perfect, and seeking to grow anyway, even though you're pretty sure you're going to fail sometimes. Nobody likes to fail. If you want to grow in your Red, you're going to blow it. But don't think of it as failure. It's just a necessary part of the growth process.

Congratulate yourself for having the courage to grow in your weak areas. And remember what Paul the Apostle said: "When I am weak, then I am strong." He had learned first-hand that God's "power is made perfect in weakness" (2 Corinthians 12:9, 10). You can learn this too, if you're willing to trust God for the power to take the risk.

Leap into the Unknown

Sometimes you're called on to take risks in the unknown. Any new situation or experience is unknown: going to a new school, joining a new organization, taking on a new responsibility. Sometimes you can draw upon past experiences to bolster your confidence: Perhaps you've moved, or joined a new club, or accepted a new responsibility before. But that doesn't completely remove the risk factor, because *this* school, club, or responsibility is different. Your options: Take the plunge, or hold back.

We encourage you to take the plunge. If you hold back in fear, you will only make it harder to risk the next time. On the other hand, if you try the new experience, you will not only learn something from that particular experience, but you will reduce your fear of trying new things in the future. You may have heard the expression, "Success breeds success." This is true because you only learn confidence by doing, by embracing new experiences.

When faced with two equally attractive college options, Jennifer chose the one that would expose her to the widest range of new experiences. It took courage to do that. But we suspect that her choice will make it easier to take other risks later on. For instance, if she's offered a job in her field that would require her to move to an unfamiliar area, she's likely to take it. If she'd gone to the other college and lived at home, she may not have developed the confidence to accept a job that would require her to move away.

These years when you are still in school are the ideal time to practice taking risks and trying new experiences. People will expect you to make mistakes; that's part of growing up. The trick is to remind yourself of this, and not feel too bad if things don't turn out ideally! Look for what you can learn from every new experience, and you'll be setting the stage for success in whatever you choose to do.

Skill #2: Connecting with People

Have you ever heard it said, "It's not what you know, it's who you know"? Usually it's said cynically, with a "sour grapes" attitude. The implication is that a person "used someone" to "get in." But in fact, "knowing the right people" is an important part of finding a job, growing on the job, succeeding on the job. People in the workplace talk a lot about it—they call it "networking." Researchers have learned that 68 percent of job hunters found their job through personal contacts. Only 9 percent got a job by answering classified ads, and only 8 percent by doing a mass mailing of their résumés and/or a letter. Career experts estimate that the vast majority of job openings go unadvertised. Why? Because chances are good that "someone knows someone who knows someone" who is perfect for the job.

Networking is not something you need to wait until you're out of school to do. Now is the time to hone this skill. If you've worked through this book, you know what your Green is. You have some idea of the career field you want to pursue. You're busy exploring your Green through your academic work, your extracurricular activities, and any interesting opportunities that come up.

As you do all that, you'll be meeting people who often share your interests and goals. Get to know these people. And not only your peers—get to know your professors too. Don't be shy about letting people know what you're doing, what you're interested in. This will be good practice for later, when you will need to let people know what kind of work you can do best. Unless people know you, they're not likely to be able to help you when you need it.

Adopt the attitude that you can learn something from everyone. Ask them about what they know, whom they know. As

DISCOVER YOUR BEST POSSIBLE FUTURE

163

you've probably observed, people are usually more than happy to talk about themselves!

Help other people when you can. And don't be afraid to ask for help from them when you need it.

This is all networking is—this give and take of information, help and good will from others. But it's amazing how many people don't do it.

We're not talking here about using people. That's not the attitude at all. When you use people, your only concern is what they can do for you. No, networking is all about helping and being helped. It's the servant's attitude that says, "I will help you in whatever way I can, and I won't be so proud that I won't accept your help if and when I need it."

Remember Jeff and the college radio station? He took the initiative to meet the person who did the sports casting because he was genuinely interested in what that person did. He learned what he could but also became a genuine friend. His new friend asked him to substitute for him sometimes when he couldn't make it to a game, and Jeff, of course, was all too happy to do so. When Jeff's friend decided to quit the job, Jeff was the natural replacement because by then he knew the job. Yes, Jeff "knew the right people." But no one felt used; everyone was helped.

Is networking only for Relationship people? Absolutely not! Admittedly, it may be easier for a Relationship person to reach out and take the initiative. But all of us need to be in touch with people—serving them, learning from them, supporting them, and receiving from them what they have to give.

If this seems like a problem for you, start small. Concentrate on being a friend to the people you already know. Treat them well, help them when you can, learn from them, ask for help when you need it. As you meet new people, do the same things. Practice, as they say, makes perfect. (And since all we're looking for is "good enough," practice will definitely make "good enough.")

Epilogue: Hard Work and a Little "Luck"

In this book we've given you guidelines for getting to know yourself and your strengths, and for practicing the skills that will increase your likelihood of finding fulfillment in a career and in life. We can't guarantee that this will lead to a wonderful career. Much depends on you—on your willingness to take the steps we've outlined, on your persistence and courage. Much also depends on circumstances outside your control—what some people call "luck."

To a Christian who believes that God is in control of everything, the idea of "luck" is suspect. Instead, the emphasis is on seeking God's will—which means first becoming more and more the kind of person God wants you to be. In Chapter 8 we talked about other principles of discovering God's will. The main point is, when we seek God with all our heart, we can trust that the opportunities and challenges ultimately come from his hand.

Even as we trust in God's providence, however, we are to do our part. According to Richard Bolles, author of the best-selling book on job hunting, *What Color Is Your Parachute?*, those who study so-called "lucky people" have discovered that lucky people have a few things in common. If you want to increase your openness to God's work in your life, note the following:

1. Providence favors those who go with their Green. People who work from their strengths and are in touch with their dreams always encounter more opportunities than those who don't know what they can do best or what they really want.

2. Providence favors those who have learned how to deal with their Red. The world is full of people who focus on what they can't do and let that limit them. "Lucky" people accept their limitations and learn how to depend on other people in the areas where they are weak and practice enough self-discipline to get things done anyway.

3. *Providence favors those who are open to new opportunities.* You've heard the saying, "Oh, that person was lucky; he was just in the right place at the right time." But is that really luck? If you generally happen to be in a lot of places a lot of the time, your chance that one of those places will be the right place is increased. And if you know your Green and have a picture of the kind of job you're looking for, you'll be able to spot "luck" (or opportunity) when it crosses your path. Also, if you're willing to take some risks as we've mentioned, you'll be more at ease with the idea of seizing "luck" when it shows up.

4. *Providence favors those who can communicate what they want and need.* Nobody can read minds. If you need a scholarship, you have to let people know of your need and you have to find out what's available. If you need a job, you have to tell people what kind of job you're looking for. If you want to help people, you have to find out what needs exist and how you can help meet them. The more people there are who know what you're looking for, the more "eyes and ears" are out there soaking up information for you; 20 ears are "luckier" than two. But you have to tell them exactly what you're looking for.

5. *Providence favors those who treat people well.* If you step on people, they tend to remember it, and they aren't above "forget-ting" to help you out when you need it. You'll tend not to be very "lucky." On the other hand, if you generously do favors for others whenever you can, they're usually happy to reciprocate. Your "luck" increases.

So here you have it—all the tips and insights we know for get-ting in touch with the way God made you and how you might be able to plug that into the work world eventually. We wish you good "luck." We wish you courage and persistence and the joy of doing what you've been designed to do. We wish you true suc-cess, not only in the job market, but in life. You'll define what that success means as you go along your own journey. But we leave you with one definition, to which we've added a postscript.

What Is Success?

To laugh often and much;

*To win the respect of intelligent people and
the affection of children;*

*To earn the appreciation of honest critics and endure
the betrayal of false friends;*

To appreciate beauty;

To find the best in others;

*To leave the world a bit better, whether by a healthy child,
a garden patch or a redeemed social condition;*

*To know even one life has breathed easier because
you have lived;*

This is to have succeeded.

—RALPH WALDO EMERSON

*And to glorify God with your life and your gifts, and
to enjoy him and his people forever—*

This is to have succeeded and to know true life.

—DIANE EBLE & DICK HAGSTROM

Resources

Books on Careers, Life Planning, and Work

Career Information Center, Fifth Edition by the Visual Education Center staff (Macmillan, 1992). Thirteen-volume set that provides information on almost any career you can imagine.

The Three Boxes of Life by Richard Nelson Bolles (Ten Speed Press, 1981). Takes a look at how to balance your life between work, learning, and leisure throughout your lifetime.

What Color Is Your Parachute? by Richard Nelson Bolles (Ten Speed Press; updated every year). This is now the classic manual for job hunting. Quite in-depth; everything you need to know about how to figure out what you want to do, where you want to do it, and how to get someone to hire you.

Your Work Matters to God by Doug Sherman and William Hendricks (NavPress, 1989). Good book on how to think about work.

Secrets of People Who Love Their Work by Janis Long Harris (InterVarsity Press, 1992). Insights of the best way to find work you love, from people in a wide range of occupations.

Books on Knowing God's Will

Decision Making by the Book by Haddon Robinson (Victor Books, 1991). Biblical principles on making wise decisions.

Finding God's Will by J. I. Packer (InterVarsity, 1985). This little booklet gives you some principles from one of the best thinkers of the Christian faith.

Knowing God's Will by Cindy Hansen (Group Books, 1990).

Knowing God's Will by M. Blaine Smith (InterVarsity, 1991). A clear discussion on basic principles of knowing God's will.

Knowing God by J. I. Packer (InterVarsity Press) and *Knowing the Face of God* by Tim Stafford (Zondervan Publishing House, 1990). These two books are more about getting to know God personally than finding his will.   As you get to know God, you tend to have a better idea of what he wants you to do.

Resources for Choosing a College

GUIDES YOU'LL FIND IN THE REFERENCE SECTION OF YOUR LIBRARY:

Barron's, Lovejoy, and *Peterson's* all publish guides for nearly every aspect of education you can think of. Consult your library or career resource center for a more complete list. To give you an example of what Peterson's offers, here is a sampling of titles:

National College Databank: The College Book of Lists. Everything you wanted to know about U.S. colleges, in list form.

Four-Year Colleges. Revised annually, this guide profiles nearly 2,000 colleges and universities, and includes important comparisons of entrance difficulty and financial aid information. Definitely one to check out at your school or local public library.

Peterson's Guide to College Admissions by R. Fred Zuker.

Two-Year Colleges. This too is updated annually, with a complete profile of every accredited two-year college.

Peterson's Choose a Christian College. Profiles all the colleges associated with the Christian College Coalition.

BOOKS

Bear's Guide to Earning Non-Traditional College Degrees by John Bear, Ph.D. (Ten Speed Press, 1988). Looks at correspondence courses, night school, summer school, weekend school, and other ways to get a degree from an accredited, but nontraditional, source.

Choosing a College by Dr. Ronald Nash (Wolgemuth & Hyatt, Publishers, 1989). Written by a Christian for Christians, it takes readers through a four-fold process, starting with asking the right questions about college to choosing possible colleges and making the final decision.

College: Getting In and Staying In by D. Bruce Lockerbie and Donald R. Fonseca (Wm. B. Eerdmans Publishing Co., 1990). Looks at the major hurdles a high-school student has to cross both to get into college and to stay there.

College: Yes or No? by William F. Shanahan (Arco Publishing, 1980). Besides helping the high-school student decide whether college is right or not for him or her, this book also looks at alternatives to a four-year college education.

Getting In! by Paulo De Oliveira and Steve Cohen (Workman, 1985). Comprehensive, from preparing for college, to applying to college, to making the decision.

How to Get Into the Right College: Secrets of College Admissions Officers by Edward B. Fiske (TimesBooks, 1988). The author conducted a national survey of college admissions officers, and here's what he came up with for advice.

The Ultimate College Shopper's Guide compiled by Heather Evans and Deidre Sullivan (Addison Wesley, 1992). Organized by lists based on personal interests, from financial aid and student life to career planning. As you decide what's most important to you in a school, this book may help you find those colleges with those characteristics.

OTHER RESOURCES ON CHOOSING A COLLEGE

Computer programs: Ask your school guidance counselor or librarian for information about computer software programs that classify colleges. This information doesn't describe or compare colleges; it doesn't pit one against another. It simply groups them, uncritically, according to various characteristics. Some we're familiar with:

The College Board's College Explorer
The College Board's College Entry
Guidance Information System
Peterson's College Selection Service

Annual college guides: Another resource is CAMPUS LIFE magazine's *College Guide.* Published in October, December and March. The October *College Guide* is geared toward helping you choose a college, with helpful articles on how to find the right college, a seasonal calendar to keep you on schedule, and helpful directories of Christian colleges and what they offer, where to write for more information, etc. The December *College Guide* focuses on financial aid, and the March guide discusses issues of college living such as getting along with roommates, looking into internships, etc. Write to: CAMPUS LIFE, 465 Gundersen Drive, Carol Stream, IL 60188. (708) 260-6200.

Books on Financial Aid

Cutting College Costs by James P. Duffy (The Career Press, 1991). If you think you can't afford a college education, pick up this book and try its suggestions.

Fund Your Way Through College by Debra M. Kirby with Christa Brelin (Visible Ink Press, 1992). Uncovers 1,100 opportunities in undergraduate financial aid.

Get Real: A Student's Guide to Money & Other Practical Matters by James Tenuto & Susan Schwartzwald (Harcourt Brace Jovanovich, Publishers, 1992).

Peterson's Paying Less For College 1993. Costs and financial aid, plus how to apply for financial aid.

Putting Your Kids Through College by Scott Edelstein and the editors of *Consumer Reports* Books (Consumer's Union, 1989). Written for parents to help finance their child's education.

Books on Student Life

How to Keep Your Faith While in College by Dr. Robert A. Morey (Crowne Publications, 1989). Written for high-school and college students, helps you develop a Christian world view as you get your education.

Surviving College Successfully by Gary DeMar (Wolgemuth & Hyatt, Publishers, 1988). Looks at learning how to survive and learning how to achieve academically.

The Truth about College by Scott Edelstein (Carol Publishing Group, 1991). Deals with problems that come up that you might not find addressed in other books, such as what to do if a teacher singles you out for ridicule or harassment, how to get an unfair grade changed, how to get out of taking an unnecessary prerequisite course.

Books on Opportunities

Learning Vacations by Gerson G. Eisenbuerg (Peterson's Guides, 1986). Another of the excellent Peterson's Guides, this one pointing you to opportunities for educational travel.

The National Directory of Internships edited by Amy S. Butterworth and Sally A. Migliore (National Society for Internships and Experiential Education, 1989). Lists opportunities in 61 fields for college, graduate, and high-school students and for adults and youth.

Summer on Campus: College Experiences for High-School Students by Shirley Levin (The College Board, 1989). A guide to opportunities to get college credit while you're still in high school.

The Teenager's Guide to Study, Travel and Adventure Abroad by the Council on International Educational Exchange ((St. Martin's Press, 1988). Information on more than 150 programs abroad, plus interviews with young people who have gone on the programs before.

Time Out: Taking a Break from School to Travel, Work & Study in the U.S. and Abroad by Robert Gilpin & Caroline Fitzgibbons (Simon & Schuster, 1992). Includes descriptions of more than 350 programs, as well as tips on preparing for a break and deciding what program is for you.

Peterson's Summer Opportunities for Kids and Teenagers

Books on Getting a Job

How to Get a Job by James Bramlett (Zondervan, 1991). Helpful book on all the basics, from finding God's will to making the grade in your new job.

How You Really Get Hired: Straight Talk for College Students from a Corporate Recruiter by John L. Lafevre (Simon & Schuster, Inc., 1989). A book that delivers on its title.

What Color Is Your Parachute? by Richard Nelson Bolles (Ten Speed Press; updated every year). This is now the classic manual for job hunting. Quite in-depth; everything you need to know about how to figure out what you want to do, where you want to do it, and how to get someone to hire you.

Who's Hiring Who?, rev. ed. by Richard Lathrop (Ten Speed Press, 1989). Another classic, focusing especially on a unique kind of résumé.